11+ Vocabulary

with

Cartoons III

By

A Mason

Cartoons by Mr. Stenly

<u>Copyright Notice</u>

Contents

This book is the **<u>third volume</u>** of the bestselling *"11+ Vocabulary Cartoons"* book *series* and has been written due to the strong demand from students, teachers and parents.

How NOT to memorize words

Vocabulary plays a big part in the 11+ exams.

A good vocabulary is inextricably linked to a good memory. To have a deep and wide vocabulary, a student needs a good memory.

The commonly accepted idea that more memorizing makes memorizing easier is **false**, and there is little truth in the popular figure of speech that likens the vocabulary memory to a muscle that grows stronger with use.

However, practice may result in an unconscious improvement in the Winning methods of memorizing.

By practice, a student comes to unconsciously discover and employ new **associative methods** in recording of facts, making them easier to recall, but we can certainly add nothing to the actual scope and power of retention.

Yet many books on memory training seek to develop the general ability to remember by incessant practice in memorizing particular words, just as one would develop a muscle by exercise.

The real cause of a poor vocabulary memory is <u>not</u> the loss of retentiveness, but the loss of an intensity of interest.

It is the failure to form sufficiently large groups and complexes of **related ideas**, emotions and muscular movements associated with the particular fact to be remembered.

Winning Strategy to build Vocabulary quickly

We recall things by their **associations**. When you set your mind to remember any particular fact, your conscious effort should not be to vaguely *will*, that it shall be impressed and retained, but analytically and deliberately connect it with other facts already in your mind.

The student who "crams" for an examination makes no permanent addition to his knowledge. There can be no recall without association, and "cramming" allows no time to form associations.

If you find it difficult to remember a word, do not waste your energies in "willing" it to return.

Try to recall some other fact associated with it.

To improve your memory you must increase the number and variety of your mental associations.

When you learn new words, make sure you learn them in a context. It is much easier to **picture a sentence** rather than picture a word in isolation.

Here is the step-by-step method that you can use to learn words quickly:

1. Link the word you are trying to learn, to another **rhyming** word or phrase.
2. Create a sentence **linking** the two words
3. Create a **mental image** for the sentence.

When you create the mental image make sure it meets **one or more of the following criteria** so that it 'sticks'.

Note: Creating an image that is memorable and 'sticky' is the Key to learning words quickly and effectively.

1. OUT OF PROPORTION - In all your images, try to distort size and shape. You can imagine things much larger than their normal size or conversely, microscopically small.

2. SUBSTITUTION - You could visualize footballers kicking a television around a football pitch instead of a football, or pens growing on a tree instead of leaves.

Substituting an out of place item in an image increases the probability of recall.

3. EXAGGERATION - Try to picture a very large quantity in your images.

4. MOVEMENT - Any movement or action is always easy to remember.

5. HUMOUR - The funnier, more absurd and zany you can make your images, the more memorable they will be.

Applying **multiple combination** of these five principles when forming your images will help make your mental associations truly outstanding and memorable.

At first, you may find that you need to **consciously apply** one or more of the five principles in order to make your pictures sufficiently ludicrous.

After a little practice however, you should find that applying the principles becomes an **automatic** and natural process.

The following words are the most common words appearing in the 11+ test and account for a majority of the difficult words that you are likely to encounter.

Each word below is illustrated with a picture using the Vocabulary building strategies listed earlier.

The pictures are provided as suggestions, and if based on your experiences/preferences, you find that you can come up with an alternative cartoon idea, please go ahead and use that.

Pronunciation Guide

The syllable breaks shown in this book reflect the pronunciation of a single word in normal speech. However, this book does not use the International Phonetic Alphabet (IPA) for pronunciation. The IPA is not very easy to understand, it is mostly for scholars and linguists. To make it easier for you to read the pronunciation, we have used the spelled pronunciation of the words.

\-\ Hyphens are used to separate syllables in pronunciation transcriptions. In actual speech, of course, there is no pause between the syllables of a word. The stress marks (bold type) indicate the stressed syllable of the word, as shown in the example below.

Interesting [*in-truh-sting*]

For one syllable words, the stress is always on the vowel and not on the consonant(s). One syllable words cannot have two stresses.

We can only stress vowels and not consonants. There are more complicated rules as to where to place the stress of a word.

For two syllable words (nouns, adjectives) the stress is placed on the first syllable. For verbs the stress is placed on the last syllable.

Example:

Nouns: **PRES**ent, **EX**port, **TA**ble

Adjectives: **PRES**ent, **CLE**ver, **HAP**py

Verbs: pre**SENT**, ex**PORT**, be**GIN**

There are many two syllable words whose meaning and class change with the change in stress. The word '*present*', for example is a two-syllable word. If we stress the first syllable, it is a noun (gift) or an adjective (opposite of absent). But if we stress the second syllable, it becomes a verb (to offer).

Use the pronunciation guide to help you pronounce a word by placing the stress on its bold syllable.

Words with Cartoons

abduct: (*ab-**duhkt***) verb

to take away by force or deception

- The detective found the man who had attempted to **abduct** the millionaire's wife.

- I recently read an exciting story about a boy who was **abducted** by aliens.

Synonyms: kidnap, seize, capture, snatch, carry off.

Antonyms: release, let go, free, liberate.

Rhyme: duck

"The Queen <u>duck</u> was <u>abducted</u> for a ransom of 100 eggs."

accentuate: (*ak-**sen**-choo-eyt*) verb

to make more noticeable and prominent; to mark something with an accent

- The blue dress she wore to the party **accentuated** her eyes.

- The film's soundtrack **accentuated** the conflicting feelings of the characters.

Synonyms: emphasize, highlight, stress, heighten, enhance.

Antonyms: diminish, mask, play down.

Rhyme: accent

"He tried to <u>accentuate</u> the danger, but his <u>accent</u> made it impossible to understand."

acclaim: (*uh-kleym*) noun, verb

public praise (n.)
to praise publicly and enthusiastically (v.)

- The actor's performance received **acclaim** from the critics. (n.)

- The summit was **acclaimed** as a great success. (v.)

Synonyms: praise, approval, applaud, commend, hail.

Antonyms: criticism, condemn, disparage, disapprove, criticise.

Rhyme: lame

"Even though the gymnast was <u>lame</u>, his performance received <u>acclaim</u>."

accord: (*uh-kawrd*) noun, verb

agreement, concurrence or harmony of things; an official agreement (n.)
to bring to an agreement; to grant someone recognition, power or status. (v.)

- The results of the study **accorded** with your hypothesis. (v.)

- Our staff members were not in **accord** with the new policy. (n.)

Synonyms: agreement, assent, consensus, harmony, treaty.

Antonyms: discord, dissent, disagreement, clash, conflict.

Rhyme: a cord

"Everyone was in <u>accord</u> that the only way to cross the ravine was by using <u>a cord</u>."

acumen: (*ah-**kyoo**-muhn*) noun

quickness of mind; the ability to make good decisions and judgements

- She demonstrated impressive political **acumen** in her essay.

- His brother had always possessed the business **acumen** to become a successful entrepreneur.

Synonyms: keenness, sharpness, shrewdness, intelligence, expertise.

Antonyms: naivety, simple-mindedness, ineptitude.

Rhyme: human

"The monkey had so much <u>acumen</u> that he was allowed to play against a <u>human</u>."

adamant: (*ad-uh-muhnt*) adjective

possessing an unshakeable resolve; not willing to change one's mind

- The young man was **adamant** about his views on the matter.

- Our professor was **adamant** that the deadline for the assignment would not be extended.

Synonyms: determined, firm, inflexible, unyielding, unwavering.

Antonyms: flexible, irresolute, lenient, compliant, amenable.

Rhyme: accident

"The <u>adamant</u> child was responsible for the <u>accident</u>."

adorn: (*uh-dawrn*) verb

to decorate or beautify

- We **adorned** our holiday tree with colourful fairy lights.

- The walls of the gallery were **adorned** with the most beautiful paintings I had ever seen.

Synonyms: beautify, decorate, embellish, enhance, garnish.

Antonyms: simplify, disfigure.

Rhyme: corn

"In the quaint village, they used <u>corn</u> to <u>adorn</u> their doors."

aggrandize: (*uh-**gran**-dahyz*) verb

to make something seem bigger, greater or more impressive

- The leader's goal was to **aggrandize** his country.

- She sought to **aggrandize** herself with her shocking stories.

Synonyms: augment, glorify, magnify.

Antonyms: decrease, diminish, humble.

Rhyme: grand prize

''The <u>grand prize</u> resulted in <u>aggrandizing</u> his medal collection.'

aggravate: (*ag-ruh-veyt*) verb

to annoy; to make something worse

- The loud ticking of the clock **aggravated** our guests.
- The patient's skin was **aggravated** by the infection.

Synonyms: annoy, frustrate, irritate, agitate, vex.

Antonyms: alleviate, appease, calm, delight, improve.

Rhyme: weight

''He aggravated his weight by eating junk food.''

agile: (*aj-ahyl*) adjective

physically or mentally quick and nimble

- To become an acrobat, you have to be incredibly **agile**.

- The ballerina was graceful and **agile** in her movements.

Synonyms: active, athletic, dexterous, sharp, swift.

Antonyms: clumsy, inactive, slow, sluggish, dull.

Rhyme: crocodile

"You have to be <u>agile</u> to outrun a <u>crocodile</u>."

aloof: (*uh-loof*) adjective

cool and reserved as opposed to forthcoming; apart or at a distance

- The new student held himself **aloof** from his classmates on the first day of school.

- My mother seemed uncharacteristically **aloof** and distant at dinner last night.

Synonyms: detached, distant, indifferent, reserved, reticent.

Antonyms: forthcoming, friendly, interested, sociable, warm.

Rhyme: roof

"He is <u>aloof</u> and prefers to party by himself on the <u>roof</u>."

amass: (*uh-mas*) verb

to gather into a pile; to come together; to collect for oneself

- The researchers had **amassed** enough evidence to come to an accurate conclusion.
- My favourite travel blogger has **amassed** an impressive following throughout the years.

Synonyms: assemble, collect, compile, gather, hoard.

Antonyms: disperse, dissipate, scatter, separate, spend.

Rhyme: grass

"The greedy cow amassed a huge pile of grass."

ambiguous: (*am-**big**-yoo-uhs*) adjective

having several possible meanings or interpretations; not clear or decided

- The wording in the contract they offered me was **ambiguous**.

- He replied with an **ambiguous** statement instead of answering me directly.

Synonyms: questionable, uncertain, vague, unclear, doubtful.

Antonyms: certain, clear, definite, determined, obvious.

Rhyme: the big bus

"When he asked the driver if <u>the big bus</u> would go to Disneyland, he gave an <u>ambiguous</u> answer."

amble: (*am-**buhl***) noun, verb

a leisurely walk; a stroll (n.)
to move at a slow, easy place, usually for pleasure (v.)

- She **ambled** along the riverbank while listening to music. (v.)

- Paris has many beautiful streets through which you can **amble**. (n.)

Synonyms: drift, meander, stroll, wander, saunter.

Antonyms: hurry, run, rush.

Rhyme: scramble

''The cool dude would only <u>amble</u> when everyone was breaking into a <u>scramble</u>.''

anguish: (*ang-gwish*) noun, verb

extreme pain or suffering (n.)
to feel or experience extreme pain, suffering or distress (v.)

- The poet expressed her **anguish** through her writing. (n.)

- He **anguished** over his failure for a few days and then decided to try again. (v.)

Synonyms: agony, torment, misery, suffering, sorrow.

Antonyms: joy, delight, pleasure, comfort, relief.

Rhyme: angry fish

''The <u>angry fish</u> caused him a lot of <u>anguish</u>.''

animated: (*an-uh-mey-tid*) adjective

full of energy, life or spirit; made to move or seem like a living thing

- My sister and I watch **animated** films every weekend.

- The director's inspiring speech **animated** the actors before the performance.

Synonyms: energetic, lively, spirited, excited, active.

Antonyms: lazy, lethargic, sluggish.

Rhyme: animals

"The tired child became <u>animated</u> when she saw the zoo <u>animals</u>."

annihilate: (*uh-**nahy**-uh-leyt*) verb

to utterly destroy or defeat

- The chess master **annihilated** his opponent during the game.

- Their troops were almost **annihilated** in the battle.

Synonyms: exterminate, crush, obliterate, vanquish, wipe out.

Antonyms: build, construct, establish, create, fix.

Rhyme: violate

''If you <u>violate</u> the law, you will be <u>annihilated</u>, said the RoboCop.''

annul: (*uh-nuhl*) verb

to revoke the legal status of a law, agreement or marriage; declare invalid

- The head of the committee has the power to **annul** any of the decisions they find inappropriate.

- After 20 years, the couple chose to **annul** their marriage.

Synonyms: cancel, abolish, delete, invalidate, revoke.

Antonyms: allow, approve, institute, legalize, pass.

Rhyme: skull

"He yelled so hard when he saw the <u>skull</u> that I had to <u>annul</u> the plans for the Haunted House."

anomaly: (*uh-**nom**-uh-lee*) noun

something or someone that is different from what is normal, expected or common

- That unfortunate incident was an **anomaly** in our company's history.

- There was an **anomaly** in the patient's blood test.

Synonyms: abnormality, oddity, deviation, inconsistency, irregularity.

Antonyms: conformity, normality, regularity, standard.

Rhyme: abnormally

"Abnormally large meteor hitting the earth is an anomaly that happens very rarely and can destroy the planet."

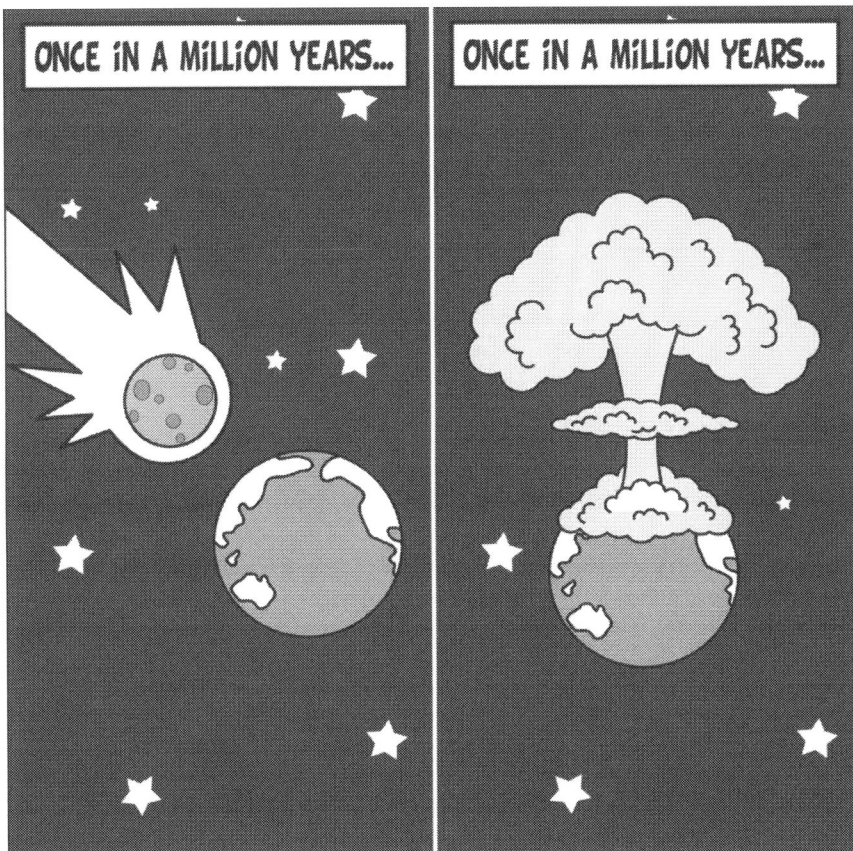

apex: (*ey-peks*) noun

the highest point of an object; the highest point of achievement

- The **apex** of the mountain was covered by a thick layer of storm clouds.

- Becoming the company President was the **apex** of his career.

Synonyms: peak, climax, summit, culmination, tip.

Antonyms: base, bottom.

Rhyme: ape x

''In the <u>ape</u> world, solving for <u>x</u> was the <u>apex</u> of intelligence.''

aplomb: (*uh-plom*) noun

unshakeable self-assurance, especially in a challenging situation

- The activist delivered her speech with great **aplomb**.
- She handled the media attention with grace and **aplomb**.

Synonyms: poise, composure, self-confidence, self-assurance.

Antonyms: insecurity, gaucheness, awkwardness.

Rhyme: bomb

''The bomb squad deactivated the <u>bomb</u> with great <u>aplomb</u>.''

applause: (*uh-plawz*) noun

showing approval or praise by clapping one's hands

- The audience greeted the dancers with enthusiastic **applause**.

- She got a round of **applause** after finishing her presentation.

Synonyms: ovation, clapping, praise.

Antonyms: booing, hissing.

Rhyme: laws

"In the ancient world, <u>laws</u> declaring everyone equal were received with great <u>applause</u>."

arduous: (*ahr-joo-us*) adjective

requiring great effort and exertion

- After a long and **arduous** journey, they finally arrived home.

- The task turned out to be more **arduous** than she had expected.

Synonyms: hard, difficult, laborious, strenuous, gruelling.

Antonyms: easy, effortless, simple.

Rhyme: are joyous

"We are joyous because the arduous race is finally over!"

assail: (*uh-seyl*) verb

to attack violently; to criticise heavily; to take on with the intention of mastering; to come upon something or someone strongly

- His new film was **assailed** by the critics.

- The pirates **assailed** the unsuspecting townspeople.

Synonyms: attack, assault, criticise, berate, bash.

Antonyms: compliment, praise, retreat, surrender.

Rhyme: mail

"Every time the mailman brings the <u>mail</u> my dog tries to <u>assail</u> him."

assemble: (*uh-**sem**-buhl*) verb

to gather into one place or unit; to bring together around a common goal;
to put together the separate parts of a machine or object

- Everyone **assembled** in the theatre for the awards ceremony.

- I like **assembling** jigsaw puzzles.

Synonyms: collect, accumulate, amass, gather, build.

Antonyms: disband, disperse, scatter, spread, take apart.

Rhyme: tremble

''When the heroes <u>assembled</u>, the villains <u>trembled</u>.''

astonish: (*uh-**ston**-ish*) verb

to surprise or impress greatly; to amaze

- She never failed to **astonish** us with her sharp wit.

- I was **astonished** to see how much my uncle had aged.

Synonyms: surprise, amaze, astound, shock, daze.

Antonyms: bore.

Rhyme: stone fish

"I was <u>astonished</u> to see the stone move. It was a <u>stone fish</u>!"

astute: (*uh-stoot*/uh-**styoot**) adjective

having keen judgement; having the ability to assess situations correctly and manipulate them to one's advantage

- With my editor's **astute** critique, I was able to improve my story.

- The band's manager made a series of **astute** business decisions that skyrocketed their success.

Synonyms: shrewd, smart, perceptive, judicious, sharp.

Antonyms: stupid, naïve, gullible, unperceptive.

Rhyme: ass in a suit

"The ass in a suit was an astute businessman."

atone: (*uh-tohn*) verb

to make amends for one's offenses or mistakes

- The criminal **atoned** for his crime.

- He asked her how he could **atone** for hurting her feelings.

Synonyms: apologize, compensate, redeem, recompense.

Antonyms: dismiss.

Rhyme: phone

''I got my aunt a shiny new <u>phone</u> to <u>atone</u> for missing her birthday party.''

attire: (*uh-**tahyur***) noun, verb

clothing, usually for formal events (n.)
to dress in clothes, especially fine or formal ones (v.)

- The cap and gown is the traditional graduation **attire**. (n.)

- The staff members at the restaurant were **attired** In festive clothing. (v.)

Synonyms: clothing, dress, outfit, costume, dress up.

Antonyms: disrobe, unclothe.

Rhyme: fire

"The Queen's flowing <u>attire</u> caught <u>fire</u> during the celebrations."

audible: (*aw-duh-buhl*) adjective

loud enough to be heard

- His voice was barely **audible** over the loud music in the room.

- I let out an **audible** sigh of relief when I finally got my test results.

Synonyms: perceptible, clear, distinct, noticeable, hearable.

Antonyms: inaudible, quiet, unclear, imperceptible, muddled.

Rhyme: old bulb

"His favourite <u>old bulb</u> made a sound that was <u>audible</u> for miles."

banquet: (*bang-kwit*) noun, verb

a lavish formal meal for many guests (n.)
to entertain with a banquet (v.)

- They victorious team were **banqueted** by the President. (v.)

- All our friends and family had gathered for an unforgettable holiday **banquet**. (n.)

Synonyms: feast, festivity, reception, meal

Antonyms: snack

Rhyme: bank quiet

"The <u>bank</u> was <u>quiet</u> because the staff were having an official <u>banquet</u>."

barrage: (*buh-rahzh*) noun, verb

heavy artillery fire used to cover a military advance on the enemy; an overwhelming number of questions aimed at someone all at once; a dam (n.) to bombard (v.)

- The Canadian troops carried out a successful **barrage** in the battle of Vimy Ridge. (n.)

- The reporters **barraged** the politicians with their incessant questions.(v.)

Synonyms: bombardment, onslaught, torrent, dam, embankment.

Antonyms: trickle.

Rhyme: massage

"The <u>barrage</u> of arrows was like a <u>massage</u> to the monster."

bask: (*bask*) verb

to lie in the warm light (usually of the sun) for pleasure and relaxation;
to enjoy and make the most of a situation

- My friends and I were **basking** in the sun at the beach.

- The winning team was **basking** in the glory of their victory.

Synonyms: enjoy, relish, savour, luxuriate, lounge.

Antonyms: work, labour, drudge, toil.

Rhyme: mask

"On sunny days, the shy boy loved to <u>bask</u> but would always wear his <u>mask</u>."

bastion: (*bas-chuhn, bas-tee-uhn*) noun

the projecting part of a fortification that is built at an angle to allow for defensive fire; something or someone that upholds values and principles

- The fortress had a **bastion** in each of its corners.

- That university remained a **bastion** of academic integrity.

Synonyms: stronghold, citadel, support, defender, upholder.

Antonyms: weakness, looseness, vulnerability, weak spot.

Rhyme: beast nation

"The <u>beast nation</u> had built a strong <u>bastion</u> that could withstand any attack."

bedraggled: (*bih-**drag**-uld*) adjective

having a dishevelled appearance.

- My cat looked absolutely **bedraggled** after her bath.

- After an exhausting day at work, her husband came home, weary and **bedraggled**.

Synonyms: dishevelled, unkempt, grubby, scruffy.

Antonyms: neat orderly, tidy, clean, fresh.

Rhyme: bedroom struggle

''The kids became <u>bedraggled</u> after the <u>bedroom struggle</u>.''

benefactor: (***ben**-uh-fak-ter*) noun

someone who invests money or other resources in a person or cause

- After his retirement, the wealthy businessman became a generous **benefactor** of the arts.

- Over the years, our kind **benefactors** have invested a great deal of money into our museum.

Synonyms: sponsor, patron, supporter, backer, promoter.

Antonyms: opponent, antagonist, adversary.

Rhyme: benefit

''The donation from the rich <u>benefactor</u> to build a new library <u>benefited</u> many students.''

benevolent: (*buh-**nev**-uh-luhnt*) adjective

expressing kindness and goodwill; charitable; serving as a charity rather than a profit-making initiative

- A **benevolent** donor paid for the girl's tuition for medical school.

- He was a **benevolent** father who wanted only the best for his children.

Synonyms: kind, generous, altruistic, well-meaning, charitable.

Antonyms: malevolent, evil, cruel, hateful, mean.

Rhyme: been violent

"The king had always <u>been violent</u> but had a change of heart and became <u>benevolent</u>."

benign: (*bih-nayn*) adjective

kindly and gracious; having no harmful effects; beneficial or pleasant

- The climate became less **benign** as we moved into the desert.

- The hostess welcomed us with a handshake and a **benign** smile.

Synonyms: mild, friendly, kind, gentle, nonthreatening.

Antonyms: harmful, harsh, malignant, violent, unkind.

Rhyme: broken spine

''He thought he had a <u>broken spine</u>, but his injury turned out to be <u>benign</u>.''

besmirch: (*bih-smirch*) verb

to make something dirty; to damage someone's reputation

- His family's good name had been **besmirched** after the public controversy.

- The white shirt was **besmirched** with mud and grime.

Synonyms: taint, tarnish, smear, slander, defame.

Antonyms: honour, praise, upgrade, clean.

Rhyme: bees march

"When the hornet <u>besmirched</u> the Queen Bee's reputation, the <u>bees marched</u> to take revenge."

bias: (*bah-uys*) noun, verb

a tendency, inclination or prejudice toward or against a person or group (n.)

cause someone to feel a prejudice toward someone or something (v.)

- Students were admitted to the college without **bias**. (n.)

- The prosecutor attempted to **bias** the jury with his speech. (v.)

Synonyms: prejudice, preference, unfairness, subjective.

Antonyms: fairness, impartiality, objective.

Rhyme: buy us

"The twins had a <u>bias</u> towards sweets and would scream '<u>buy us</u>' whenever they passed a sweet shop."

blandishment: (*blan-dish-muhnt*) noun

flattery that is used to persuade someone to do something

- He charmed the committee with his **blandishments**.

- As the head of a major company, she was no stranger to **blandishments** and false promises.

Synonyms: flattery, fawning, adulation, sweet talk, praise.

Antonyms: criticism, critique, judgement.

Rhyme: bland dish meant

"The <u>bland dish meant</u> that the child would need lots of <u>blandishment</u>."

blemish: (*blem-ish*) noun, verb

a small flaw that ruins the perfection of something; a fault or defect (n.)

to damage or ruin the quality or appearance of something (v.)

- The teenage girl had a large **blemish** on the tip of her nose. (n.)
- The student's flawless record was **blemished** by a minor offense. (v.)

Synonyms: mark, pimple, stain, damage, tarnish.

Antonyms: blank, clarity, perfection, embellishment, restore.

Rhyme: blame fish

"Her immaculate dress was <u>blemished,</u> and she <u>blamed</u> it on the <u>fish</u>."

bliss: (*bliss*) noun

a state of supreme joy; heaven, paradise (n.)
to reach a state of supreme joy (v.)

- The old couple had shared 50 years of **bliss** together.

- Their idea of **bliss** is swimming in the lake on a hot summer's day.

Synonyms: happiness, ecstasy, joy, paradise, euphoria.

Antonyms: depression, misery, sadness, sorrow, woe.

Rhyme: hiss

''He was in a state of <u>bliss</u> when he could no longer hear the <u>hiss</u>.''

bounty: (*boun-tee*) noun

a generous reward for capturing or killing someone; occurring in generous amount; generosity in giving

- A large **bounty** was offered for the capture of the villain.

- The charity depends on the **bounty** of its contributors.

Synonyms: abundance, plenty, generosity, donation, reward.

Antonyms: scarcity, penalty, punishment.

Rhyme: bound to tree

"He <u>bound</u> the bandit to a <u>tree</u> and received the <u>bounty</u>."

brazen: (*brey-zuhn*) adjective

bold and shameless

- He had never shown such a **brazen** disregard for other's feelings.
- I was always struck by her ability to tell such **brazen** lies.

Synonyms: bold, shameless, audacious, bold, blatant.

Antonyms: humble, meek, modest, timid, shy.

Rhyme: brays on

''The brazen donkey brays on at night, disturbing the other animals trying to sleep.''

breach: (*breech*) noun, verb

a break or rupture; violation of a law or a promise; a gap made in a wall (n.)
to break or rupture; to break a law or a promise (v.)

- The company was sued when they **breached** the contract. (v.)

- Over the years, the **breach** between them grew wider and wider until they felt like strangers again. (n.)

Synonyms: opening, break, hole, violation, infringe.

Antonyms: closing, closure, juncture, agreement, honour.

Rhyme: beach

"The large river <u>breached</u> the dam and flooded the river <u>beach</u>."

cache: (*kash*) noun, verb

a hiding or storage place for something; something hidden in a hiding place (n.)
to hide, conceal or put in a cache (v.)

- The boy keeps his treasures in a secret **cache** beneath his bed. (n.)

- They decided to **cache** their money somewhere where no one would ever find it. (v.)

Synonyms: hideout, hideaway, collection, storehouse, hide.

Antonyms: spend, discard, waste.

Rhyme: cash

"The robbers <u>cached</u> the stolen <u>cash</u> on a tree, but the storm blew it away."

callous: (*kal-uhs*) adjective

lacking in sympathy for others; indifferent to the feelings and needs of other people; insensitive; hardened

- His **callous** attitude at work made him unpopular.

- Her behaviour toward their dinner guests was rude and **callous**.

Synonyms: heartless, unfeeling, insensitive, indifferent, unsympathetic.

Antonyms: caring, compassionate, kind, sympathetic, mindful.

Rhyme: palace

"The callous queen lived in a huge palace and did not care for her people."

capitulate: (*kah-**pich**-uh-leyt*) verb

to stop resisting; to surrender on someone else's terms

- We refused to **capitulate** to their unreasonable demands.

- After a long argument, he finally **capitulated** to his mother's wishes.

Synonyms: surrender, submit, yield, concede, relent.

Antonyms: resist, withstand, conquer, defend.

Rhyme: congratulate

''The Captain <u>congratulated</u> his men when the enemy finally <u>capitulated</u>.''

castigate: (*kas-ti-geyt*) verb

to criticise someone severely; to punish someone, usually with the intention of correcting their behaviour

- The boy knew that his parents would **castigate** him for his behaviour when he got home.

- She was unfairly **castigated** in the news article.

Synonyms: criticise, scold, reprimand, chastise, punish.

Antonyms: approve, compliment, flatter, praise, forgive.

Rhyme: gate

"They were <u>castigated</u> for breaking the school <u>gate</u>."

catapult: (*kat-uh-pult*) noun, verb

a device used to hurl or launch an object across a wide distance (n.)

to launch something, usually with a catapult; to move quickly and suddenly (v.)

- Their experimental album **catapulted** the band to the top of the charts. (v.)

- Ancient **catapults** were made of wood and iron. (n.)

Synonyms: launcher, propeller, hurl, throw, shoot.

Antonyms: There are no antonyms for the word Catapult.

Rhyme: cats pulled

''The cats pulled hard at the catapult to destroy their enemies for good.''

cease: (*sees*) verb

to stop; to come to an end

- His talent never **ceases** to amaze me.

- The general ordered his troops to **cease** fire.

Synonyms: stop, end, discontinue, conclude, terminate.

Antonyms: begin, continue, complete, persevere, commence.

Rhyme: seize

"His phone was <u>seized</u> when he did not <u>cease</u> using it in class."

celerity: (*suh-**ler**-i-tee*) noun

speed or swiftness of movement

- The **celerity** of their movement as they raced through the woods was astounding.
- **Celerity** was never his priority when it came to making life-changing decisions.

Synonyms: speed, rapidity, swiftness, briskness, haste.

Antonyms: slowness, sluggishness, delay.

Rhyme: celery

"The <u>celery</u> plant moved with <u>celerity</u>."

chandelier: (*shan-dl-eer*) noun

a large ornate light that hangs from the ceiling, usually having branches for multiple lightbulbs or candles.

- A beautiful glass **chandelier** was hanging in the ballroom.

- The musical begins with a massive **chandelier** falling from the ceiling.

Synonyms: lamp, candelabra, arc light.

Antonyms: There are no antonyms for the word Chandelier.

Rhyme: candle here

''Put the <u>candles here</u>, said the queen pointing at the <u>chandelier</u>.''

chaos: (*key-os*) noun

a state of complete disorder; an absolute lack of organization; total confusion;

- The boy's bedroom was in a state of utter **chaos**.
- Last night's snowstorm caused **chaos** on the roads.

Synonyms: disorder, confusion, disarray, pandemonium, anarchy.

Antonyms: order, harmony, orderliness, peace, organization.

Rhyme: Key Loss

''The Key loss meant there was chaos at the airport.''

clemency: (*klem-uhn-see*) noun

an act of forgiveness or mercy

- After hearing the jury's verdict, the defendant appealed to the judge for **clemency**.

- After 15 years of serving a prison sentence, she was granted **clemency**.

Synonyms: mercy, compassion, pity, leniency, grace.

Antonyms: cruelty, meanness, mercilessness.

Rhyme: lemon tea

"The lemon king showed no <u>clemency</u> and ordered all criminal lemons to be turned into <u>lemon tea</u>."

collude: (*kuh-lood*) verb

to work together in secret, especially in an unlawful or immoral way

- The crew was **colluding** to take over the ship.

- He was **colluding** with their rivals the entire time.

Synonyms: conspire, plot, scheme, connive, machinate.

Antonyms: forget, neglect.

Rhyme: cat food

''The mice <u>colluded</u> to steal the <u>cat's food</u>.''

colossal: (*kuh-los-uhl*) adjective

extremely large in size

- After the banquet, they were left with a **colossal** mess to clean up.

- Declining that job offer was a **colossal** mistake.

Synonyms: enormous, gigantic, huge, immense, gargantuan.

Antonyms: small, tiny, little, miniature, miniscule.

Rhyme: fossil

"The anthropologist found a <u>colossal</u> dinosaur <u>fossil</u> in the ice."

commiseration: (*kuh-miz-uh-**rey**-shuhn*) noun

the process of empathizing with someone's grief, sorrow or pain

- You have all of my sympathy and **commiseration**.

- She offered her friend words of **commiseration** for her loss.

Synonyms: pity, sympathy, condolence, compassion.

Antonyms: disdain, indifference, mercilessness.

Rhyme: train station

''I offered my <u>commiseration</u> when he missed his last <u>train</u> at the <u>station</u>.''

complacent: (*kuhm-**pley**-suhnt*) adjective

being uncritically self-satisfied; being smug

- After years of hard work, the designer has become **complacent** in his career.

- She wants to keep striving for something greater instead of growing **complacent**.

Synonyms: satisfied, content, smug, unworried, pleased.

Antonyms: unhappy, discontent, dissatisfied, concerned, anxious.

Rhyme: compliment

"The star athlete became <u>complacent</u> after receiving many <u>compliments</u>."

concave: (*kon-keyv*) adjective

curved inwards like the inside of a hollow sphere

- The **concave** side of the bowl was covered in intricate hand-painted flowers.
- He was prescribed **concave** contact lenses to help with his short-sightedness.

Synonyms: bowl-shaped, dented, hollow, curved in, dipped.

Antonyms: convex, distended, straight.

Rhyme: wave

''The best surfing <u>wave</u> is <u>concave</u>.''

conciliation: (*kuhn-si-lee-ey-shn*) noun

the act of helping two parties resolve a dispute; the act of placating someone

- While the first attempt at **conciliation** between them had failed, the second one was a success.

- The person mediating a **conciliation** must remain impartial.

Synonyms: appeasement, pacification, reunion, placation.

Antonyms: provocation, alienation, estrangement, separation.

Rhyme: humiliation

"He chose <u>conciliation</u> over <u>humiliation</u>."

concur: (*kuhn-kur*) verb

to agree in opinion; to cooperate; to take place at the same time

- I strongly **concur** with your ideas on that issue and will help you come up with an effective solution.

- He enjoys holding discussions with people whose beliefs do not **concur** with his own.

Synonyms: agree, coincide, correspond, harmonize, assent.

Antonyms: disagree, clash, dissent, oppose, protest.

Rhyme: concorde

''Everybody <u>concurs</u> that the supersonic <u>concorde</u> was the fastest commercial flight between London and New York.''

confound: (*kon-found*) verb

to confuse or surprise someone; to prove something false; to defeat or overthrow

- The complicated instructions **confounded** him.

- The magician **confounded** the audience with his mind-boggling magic tricks.

Synonyms: confuse, mistake, stun, amaze, puzzle, defeat.

Antonyms: bore, clarify, enlighten, explain.

Rhyme: con found

"After <u>confounding</u> the police for several years, the <u>con</u> was <u>found</u> hiding in a monastery."

conjecture: (*kuhn-jek-cher*) noun, verb

conclusion formed based on incomplete evidence; an unproven theory (n.)

to form an opinion or conclusion based on incomplete information (v.)

- Though he argued confidently, most of his points were pure **conjecture**. (n.)

- The students **conjectured** about the topics that would be tested in the examination. (v.)

Synonyms: guess, estimation, speculation, estimate, infer

Antonyms: fact, truth.

Rhyme: confusing lecture

''After the <u>confusing lecture</u>, the students could only <u>conjecture</u> on what was taught!''

consent: (*kuhn-sent*) noun, verb

permission or approval; agreement in opinion or feeling (n.)

to give permission or approval; to agree (v.)

- We did not **consent** to their terms. (v.)

- They asked the workers for their written **consent** to appear in the documentary. (n.)

Synonyms: agreement, permission, approval, agree, allow.

Antonyms: refusal, decline, forbid, reject.

Rhyme: content

"The suspicious passenger refused to give <u>consent</u> to have his bag's <u>contents</u> checked."

conundrum: (*kuh-**nuhn**-druhm*) noun

something that confuses, such as a riddle, a puzzle or a problem; a difficult situation

- The professors were faced with a serious moral **conundrum**.

- Finding the perfect Halloween costume was proving to be a **conundrum**.

Synonyms: problem, difficulty, dilemma, puzzle, enigma, riddle.

Antonyms: clarification, solution.

Rhyme: canon drum

'' When their drum broke, the music group used a <u>canon drum</u> to resolve their <u>conundrum</u>.''

daunting: (*dahn-ting*) adjective

challenging to overcome; causing discouragement or fear in someone

- Speaking in front of an audience can be **daunting**, but you can improve your skills with practice.

- Traveling abroad by herself for the first time seemed **daunting** even though she wanted to go.

Synonyms: intimidating, unnerving, discouraging, scary, tough.

Antonyms: comfortable, easy, heartening.

Rhyme: taunting

''Although the bully was <u>daunting</u>, he could not take the <u>taunting</u> anymore and struck him.''

debacle: (*dey-**bah**-kuhl*) noun

a sudden, and often, humiliating failure; a fiasco

- The sequel to the film was a total **debacle**.

- She needed some time to recover from her recent **debacle** at work.

Synonyms: disaster, catastrophe, fiasco, tragedy, devastation.

Antonyms: success, accomplishment, victory, triumph, attainment.

Rhyme: the buckle

"The reason for the <u>debacle</u> was that he forgot to fasten the <u>buckle</u>."

deplore: (*dih-plohr*) verb

to feel or express strong disapproval; to feel or express intense regret

- He **deplores** people who do not care about others.

- We strongly **deplore** the use of insults in a live debate.

Synonyms: condemn, criticise, abhor, regret, lament.

Antonyms: approve, praise, commend, esteem, favour.

Rhyme: dance floor

"The teachers deplored that the dance floor was broken by unruly students."

deride: (*dih-rahyd*) verb

to ridicule, mock or express contempt for

- Instead of **deriding** her work, you could have offered some constructive feedback.

- She bravely stood up to the bullies who were **deriding** her clothing.

Synonyms: mock, ridicule, disdain, scoff, knock.

Antonyms: approve, admire, praise, flatter, compliment.

Rhyme: deer ride

"The deer riders were derided by others."

detest: (*dih-test*) verb

to feel strong dislike for something

- I **detest** waking up early; I prefer to sleep in.

- My son **detests** any form of animal cruelty.

Synonyms: hate, loathe, despise, abhor, dislike.

Antonyms: love, adore, like, appreciate, enjoy.

Rhyme: retest

"I <u>detest</u> the <u>retest</u> but had no option since I failed the first time around."

dexterous: (*dek-ster-uhs*) adjective

having or demonstrating skill, especially with one's hands

- As we age, our bodies become less **dexterous**.

- He is a **dexterous** electric guitarist.

Synonyms: able, adept, agile, nimble, deft.

Antonyms: clumsy, awkward, inept, blundering.

Rhyme: disastrous

''She was <u>dexterous</u> at the piano, but <u>disastrous</u> at skating.''

disconcerted: (*dis-kuhn-**sur**-tid*) adjective

bewildered, disturbed or confused, usually by something unexpected

- He was **disconcerted** to find that he missed his flight.

- Tim's parents were **disconcerted** when he did not return from school at the usual time.

Synonyms: unsettled, baffled, perturbed, upset, agitated.

Antonyms: composed, relaxed, assured.

Rhyme: concert

"The abrupt change in weather <u>disconcerted</u> the audience in the <u>concert</u>."

dogma: (*dawg-muh*) noun

beliefs or principles proclaimed to be indisputably true, usually by a system or an authority

- He prefers to think critically and hear different points of view, instead of relying on **dogma**.

- An unexamined opinion can become a **dogma**.

Synonyms: doctrine, belief, tenet, creed, philosophy.

Antonyms: There are no antonyms for the word Dogma.

Rhyme: dog ma

"The great old Dog Ma spread the dogma."

dogmatic: (*dawg-**mat**-ik*) adjective

inclined to asserting certain beliefs, opinions and principles as unquestionably true

- He had rigidly **dogmatic** views on that subject.

- The philosopher's **dogmatic** ideas did not resonate with the public.

Synonyms: rigid, intolerant, inflexible, assertive, stubborn.

Antonyms: open-minded, flexible, tolerant, impartial.

Rhyme: dramatic

"My dog was <u>dogmatic</u> about chasing cats but one day, he underwent a <u>dramatic</u> change and became friends with the cats."

doleful: (*dohl-ful*) adjective

sorrowful, mournful or melancholy

- She moped about the house all day in a **doleful** manner.

- His **doleful** poetry beautifully captures the essence of
  hoartbreak.

Synonyms: unhappy, miserable, woeful, gloomy, mournful.

Antonyms: happy, cheerful, jolly, joyful, gleeful.

Rhyme: doll full

"She became <u>doleful</u> when she saw the empty box that used to be
<u>full</u> of <u>dolls</u>."

domicile: (*dom-uh-sahyl*/ *dom-uh-suhl*) noun

legal place of residence; a dwelling place

- The visa application required me to mention my occupation and **domicile**.

- A person's **domicile** is not always the same as their nationality.

Synonyms: residence, house, abode, dwelling.

Antonyms: homelessness.

Rhyme: missile

"Their <u>domicile</u> was destroyed by a misguided <u>missile</u>."

drench: (*drench*) verb

to wet or soak fully; to immerse in liquid

- Sam fell in the big puddle and was **drenched**.

- After her vigorous workout, her face was **drenched** with sweat.

Synonyms: soak, wet, saturate, douse, inundate.

Antonyms: dry, dehydrate, parch.

Rhyme: French

''During our <u>French</u> tour, we were <u>drenched</u> because of sudden rain.''

eccentric: (*ik-cen-trik*) adjective, noun

unconventional or a little strange; not placed in the centre (adj.)
a person with an unusual or unconventional personality (n.)

- The old man was an **eccentric** who liked to collect empty milk cartons. (n.)

- The writer was a bit **eccentric**, but his novels were truly brilliant. (adj.)

Synonyms: unconventional, peculiar, unusual, strange, oddball.

Antonyms: conventional, normal, typical, usual, traditional.

Rhyme: egg-centric

'The eccentric man followed an egg-centric life.''

ecstatic: (*ek-**stat**-ik*) adjective

in a state of ecstasy; feeling extreme joy and excitement

- I was **ecstatic** when I heard the good news.

- We were **ecstatic** at the idea of going on vacation.

Synonyms: overjoyed, delighted, elated, euphoric, blissful.

Antonyms: miserable, down, dejected, woeful.

Rhyme: static

"When his <u>static</u> car moved, he became <u>ecstatic</u>."

edict: (*ee-dikt*) noun

an official decree or proclamation issued by an authority

- The emperor's **edict** forbade anyone from leaving the city.

- The new **edict** could be interpreted in many ways.

Synonyms: proclamation, decree, directive, pronouncement, law.

Antonyms: appeal, request.

Rhyme: addict

"The school issued an <u>edict</u> banning phones as everyone seemed to be turning into a phone <u>addict</u>."

eerie: (eer-ee) adjective

strange and scary

- We walked down the **eerie** path through the alleyway.

- The woods look **eerie** at night.

Synonyms: creepy, spooky, uncanny, unnerving, scary.

Antonyms: normal, familiar, common, natural, regular.

Rhyme: Siri

''The forest was so <u>eerie</u> that I asked <u>Siri</u> to help me get out.''

effrontery: (*ih-**fruhn**-tuh-ree*) noun

rude or shameless boldness

- She had the **effrontery** to accuse me of lying.

- He does not have the **effrontery** to return here after what he did.

Synonyms: arrogance, impudence, nerve, audacity, disrespect.

Antonyms: carefulness, caution, modesty, meekness, politeness.

Rhyme: cemetery

"It is an <u>effrontery</u> to play loud music in a <u>cemetery</u>."

egregious: (*ih-**gree**-juhs*) adjective

extremely bad or shocking

- They made **egregious** and impossible demands, so we chose to stop working with them.

- The news story seemed too **egregious** to be true.

Synonyms: atrocious, deplorable, appalling, shocking, intolerable.

Antonyms: good, mild, slight, minor, little.

Rhyme: eggs at us

"The performance was so <u>egregious</u> that the audience threw <u>eggs at us</u>."

elated: (*ih-ley-tid*) adjective

incredibly happy or proud

- We were **elated** by his hard-earned success.

- I felt **elated** when I saw her again after so many years.

Synonyms: ecstatic, overjoyed, thrilled, delighted, excited.

Antonyms: desolate, disheartened, discouraged, dejected, deflated.

Rhyme: baited

''He was <u>elated</u> when he <u>baited</u> a big fish.''

elation: (*ih-ley-shuhn*) noun

a feeling of great joy or pride

- The audience clapped and cheered with **elation**.

- She felt a strange sense of **elation** at the thought of moving to a new city.

Synonyms: ecstasy, joy, delight, euphoria, excitement.

Antonyms: sadness, despair, misery, desolation, depression.

Rhyme: election

''His <u>elation</u> knew no bounds after he won the school <u>election</u>.''

emaciated: (*ih-**mey**-shee-ey-tid*) adjective

extremely thin, usually due to an illness or a lack of food

- After his illness, the boy was completely **emaciated**.

- Her **emaciated** body was shivering in the cold.

Synonyms: skeletal, withered, shrunken, scrawny, skinny.

Antonyms: plump, fat, chubby, overweight, thick.

Rhyme: contaminated

"The water was <u>contaminated</u>, and the polar bear became <u>emaciated</u> being unable to find anything edible."

emulate: (*em-yuh-leyt*) verb

to imitate in order to match or surpass a person or achievement

- Many young entrepreneurs try to **emulate** Steve Job's path to success instead of finding their own way.

- She wanted to **emulate** the style of her favourite filmmaker.

Synonyms: imitate, mimic, mirror, compete, rival.

Antonyms: neglect, spurn.

Rhyme: I am late

"I am late because I tried to emulate my superhero, said the boy."

encrypt: (*en-kript*) verb

to convert data or information into code to prevent unauthorised access

- There was a secret message **encrypted** into the painting.

- He uses a special technique to **encrypt** his account details.

Synonyms: encode, inscribe, hide, conceal, encipher.

Antonyms: decode, decipher, decrypt.

Rhyme: Egypt

''The pharaoh's tomb in <u>Egypt</u> had <u>encrypted</u> script that supposedly led to the hidden treasure.''

encumber: (*en-**kum**-ber*) verb

to block or impede the free movement of something or someone; to burden with obligations, debt etc.

- Their company is **encumbered** by a massive debt.

- The extra suitcase will **encumber** me on my trip.

Synonyms: burden, block, hinder, impede, inconvenience.

Antonyms: unburden, unblock, aid, assist.

Rhyme: cucumber

"His cucumber business was encumbered with debt."

endeavour: (*en-**deh**-vuhr*) noun, verb

an attempt (n.)
to attempt to do something (v.)

- We will **endeavour** to arrange a meeting for you. (v.)

- It was an honest **endeavour** to make a difference in the community. (n.)

Synonyms: try, attempt, enterprise, effort, undertaking.

Antonyms: forget, ignore, neglect, idle, rest.

Rhyme: diver

"The diver's endeavour finally led to finding the treasure."

endorse: (*en-dawrs*) verb

to publicly declare approval or support of; to recommend something in an advertisement; to sign one's name on a document

- No one wanted to **endorse** his unrealistic plan.

- The actress was thrilled to **endorse** her favourite makeup brand.

Synonyms: approve, advocate, champion, sanction, authorise.

Antonyms: reject, oppose, criticise, invalidate, disapprove.

Rhyme: horse

"The champion <u>horse</u> <u>endorsed</u> the 'Run Faster' product."

enhance: (*en-hans*) verb

to improve the quality of; to elevate to a higher degree

- The new camera will **enhance** the quality of her videos.

- Those colours **enhanced** her natural beauty.

Synonyms: improve, augment, enrich, heighten, increase.

Antonyms: decrease, diminish, lesson, worsen, minimize.

Rhyme: France

"I decided to move to <u>France</u> in order to <u>enhance</u> my French skill."

enigmatic: (*en-ig-**mat**-ik*) adjective

mysterious; difficult to understand or interpret

- His answers to my questions were suspiciously **enigmatic**.

- The model had an **enigmatic** smile that captivated people's attention.

Synonyms: mysterious, unknowable, puzzling, inexplicable, ambiguous.

Antonyms: clear, obvious, straightforward, plain, explicit.

Rhyme: mathematic

"I found the advanced <u>mathematics</u> class a bit <u>enigmatic</u>."

equitable: (*ek-wi-tuh-buhl*) adjective

fair and equal; impartial

- The current economic system is not **equitable**.

- Every member of the team deserves to have an **equitable** share of the profits.

Synonyms: reasonable, fair, unbiased, just, impartial.

Antonyms: unfair, unjust, unreasonable, partial, biased.

Rhyme: equal table

''As part of the <u>equitable</u> settlement, all heirs received an <u>equal</u> part of the Royal <u>table</u>.''

erode: (*ih-rohd*) verb

to gradually wear away by wind, water or sand; to slowly destroy

- Over time, the river **eroded** a deep gorge in that area.

- Time will not **erode** his most beautiful memories of his children.

Synonyms: corrode, wear away, grind down, eat away, destroy.

Antonyms: build, preserve, maintain, construct, rebuild.

Rhyme: road

"The downpour was so strong that the <u>road</u> was <u>eroded</u>."

esteem: (*ih-steem*) noun, verb

respect and admiration for something or someone (n.)
to regard favourably; to regard someone with respect and admiration (v.)

- Her friends and teammates hold her in high **esteem**. (n.)

- His academic works are **esteemed** very highly by experts. (v.)

Synonyms: honour, reverence, respect, value, admire.

Antonyms: contempt, disregard, disrespect, scorn, condemn.

Rhyme: team

"The top scorer was held in <u>esteem</u> by his basketball <u>team</u>."

euphoric: (*yoo-fawr-ik*) adjective

extremely happy or excited

- I felt **euphoric** after seeing my favourite band perform live.

- Their **euphoric** laughter resonated throughout the entire building.

Synonyms: overjoyed, elated, ecstatic, enraptured, excited.

Antonyms: bored, depressed, sober, calm, despairing.

Rhyme: heroic

''I felt <u>euphoric</u> when my <u>heroic</u> friend dived in to save the child.''

evade: (*ih-veyd*) verb

to avoid or escape by using deceit and trickery; to avoid answering directly; to avoid dealing with something

- The actor cleverly **evaded** all the invasive questions at the press conference.

- She always manages to **evade** her responsibilities at work.

Synonyms: avoid, dodge, elude, sidestep, circumvent.

Antonyms: confront, face, disclose.

Rhyme: parade

"He tried to <u>evade</u> the cops by mingling with the <u>parade</u>."

exalted: (*ig-**zawl**-tid*) adjective

elevated in status or rank; having a high station; of a noble or lofty nature; extremely happy

- The young boys felt **exalted** when their team won.

- The new managers were enjoying their newly **exalted** status.

Synonyms: elevated, honoured, promoted, illustrious, lofty.

Antonyms: lowly, unimportant, disparaged, criticised, belittled.

Rhyme: halted

"He was <u>halted</u> before he could enter the area meant for the <u>exalted</u> guests."

exasperated: (*ig-**zas**-puh-rey-tid*) adjective

extremely annoyed, irritated or frustrated

- I was **exasperated** by their incessant chatter.

- The more he watched that show, the more **exasperated** he became.

Synonyms: annoyed, irritated, frustrated, infuriated, enraged.

Antonyms: appeased, placated, composed, pacified.

Rhyme: separated

''She was <u>exasperated</u> when she got <u>separated</u> from her child at the fun fair.''

expel: (*ik-spel*) verb

to remove someone from school or an organization; to force someone to leave a place; to push something out, usually from the body

- If he had been caught, he would have been **expelled** from college.

- When we exhale, we **expel** carbon dioxide from our lungs.

Synonyms: eject, dislodge, discharge, remove.

Antonyms: absorb, admit, take in.

Rhyme: spell

''He could not <u>spell</u> so he was <u>expelled</u> from the class''

exult: (*ig-zuhlt*) verb

to feel or express triumphant joy and elation

- Our national team **exulted** over their victory.

- The young scientist **exulted** in her new discovery.

Synonyms: revel, triumph, rejoice, celebrate.

Antonyms: lament, grieve, mourn, conceal.

Rhyme: insult

''He <u>exulted</u> when he avenged his <u>insult</u>.''

fallow: (*fal-oh*) adjective, noun

inactive or unproductive; (of land) ploughed but left unseeded (adj.)
a piece of unseeded land (n.)

- The fields were left **fallow** over the summer.

- After a year-long **fallow** period, she went back to writing her book.

Synonyms: unplanted, uncultivated, unseeded, unproductive.

Antonyms: creative, cultivated, productive, active, used.

Rhyme: follow

"The fields lay <u>fallow</u> because the novice farmer could not <u>follow</u> instructions."

fastidious: (*fa-stid-ee-uhs*) adjective

extremely concerned with details, accuracy and cleanliness

- She had always been **fastidious** about the way she dressed.

- After his surgery, Ryan became **fastidious** about his health.

Synonyms: picky, meticulous, exacting, fussy, detail oriented.

Antonyms: easy-going, carefree, indifferent.

Rhyme: tedious

''The <u>fastidious</u> teacher made the boring task even more <u>tedious</u>.''

fawning: (*fah-nuhng*) adjective

showing exaggerated flattery, admiration or affection

- At the height of his popularity, everyone was **fawning** over him.

- She didn't enjoy people **fawning** over her.

Synonyms: flattering, submissive, ingratiating, servile.

Antonyms: aloof, assertive, proud.

Rhyme: frowning

"The <u>fawning</u> turned to <u>frowning</u> when they realised that he was a cheat."

fealty: (*fee-uhl-tee*) noun

a formal oath of loyalty sworn to a lord

- The knights swore **fealty** to their king.

- He pledged his **fealty** to his lord.

Synonyms: loyalty, faithfulness, devotion, fidelity, duty.

Antonyms: disloyalty, unfaithfulness, treachery, betrayal.

Rhyme: feel tree

"Everyone who swore <u>fealty</u> to the Chief had to <u>feel</u> the sacred <u>tree</u>."

feat: (*feet*) noun

a remarkable or extraordinary act or accomplishment, especially one that takes courage and skill

- Staging a successful musical is no easy **feat**.

- This building is an incredible **feat** of engineering.

Synonyms: achievement, accomplishment, deed, act.

Antonyms: failure, defeat, forfeit.

Rhyme: feet

"He completed the feat of walking around the world in his bare feet!"

fickle: (*fik-uhl*) adjective

frequently changing one's mind, loyalties and affections

- The fashion industry is notoriously **fickle**.

- She is very **fickle** when it comes to her career.

Synonyms: volatile, capricious, changeable, unpredictable, flighty.

Antonyms: stable, constant, consistent, reliable, predictable.

Rhyme: pickle

"He was so <u>fickle</u> that he could not decide on the <u>pickle</u>."

fidget: (*fij-it*) verb

to move about or play with something nervously or restlessly

- The children could not sit still; they were **fidgeting** the whole time.
- I was so nervous before the meeting that I kept **fidgeting** with my bracelets.

Synonyms: fiddle, fret, squirm, twitch, twiddle.

Antonyms: rest, relax, be still.

Rhyme: midget

"The <u>midget</u> would constantly <u>fidget</u> preventing others from enjoying the film."

flaccid: (*flas*-id/ *flak*-sid) adjective

soft and limp; weak

- His face was naïve and **flaccid**.

- The seatbelts in his car were worn and **flaccid**.

Synonyms: limp, soft, flabby, drooping, lifeless.

Antonyms: firm, tight, taught.

Rhyme: fatty acid

"His tummy became <u>flaccid</u> due to eating food with too much <u>fatty acid</u>."

flaunt: (*flawnt*) verb

to display something or someone ostentatiously, usually to get admiration, inspire envy or show defiance

- They **flaunted** their wealth with their expensive clothes and luxury cars.

- She was too humble to **flaunt** her success.

Synonyms: exhibit, display, parade, brandish, show off.

Antonyms: hide, conceal, cover, withhold, suppress.

Rhyme: flying aunt

''Her <u>flying aunt</u> liked to <u>flaunt</u> her abilities.''

flout: (*flout*) verb

openly disobey or disregard a rule or law

- People **flout** traffic laws far too often in this town.

- The cyclist was **flouting** the law by refusing to wear a helmet.

Synonyms: defy, disregard, disobey, ignore, scoff.

Antonyms: approve, commend, please, honour, respect.

Rhyme: shout

"He <u>flouted</u> the rules by <u>shouting</u>."

forthright: (*fohrth*-*rahyt*) adjective

frank and outspoken; getting straight to the point when speaking

- Because she is so refreshingly **forthright**, you always know where you stand with her.

- Our manager's **forthright** manner of speaking is often mistaken for arrogance.

Synonyms: upfront, direct, straightforward, frank, blunt.

Antonyms: timid, tactful, devious, sly, secretive.

Rhyme: fork right

"The forthright waiter at the expensive restaurant reminded us how to hold the fork right while eating."

frenzy: (*fren-zee*) noun

a state or period of wild excitement, agitation or behaviour

- She tore through the drawers in a **frenzy**, trying to find the letter.

- The child was in a **frenzy** when he could not find his toy.

Synonyms: craze, fever, turmoil, passion, flurry.

Antonyms: calm, order, peace, harmony, balance.

Rhyme: friendly

"The fish seemed <u>friendly</u>, till they started their feeding <u>frenzy</u>."

gape: (*geyp*) noun, verb

a wide opening; a widely open mouth; a yawn (n.)
to stare with one's mouth wide open, as if in amazement; to open (v.)

- The huge **gape** of the animal's jaws scared the little kids. (n.)

- Everyone was **gaping** at her outfit as she was walking down the street. (v.)

Synonyms: stare, gawk, separate, divide.

Antonyms: ignore, close.

Rhyme: ape

'' On the planet of the <u>apes</u>, the apes <u>gaped</u> at the only human.''

glee: (*glee*) noun

great delight or pleasure

- Our daughter opened her birthday presents with excitement and **glee**.

- She couldn't help shouting out with **glee**.

Synonyms: delight, elation, joy, pleasure, triumph.

Antonyms: depression, melancholy, pain, sorrow, misery.

Rhyme: glowing jelly

''She reacted with <u>glee</u> when presented with <u>glowing jelly</u>.''

glitch: (*glich*) noun

a defect, error or malfunction

- My computer has a **glitch**, so I got a technician to fix it.

- There was a minor **glitch** in the system.

Synonyms: malfunction, error, bug, problem, flaw.

Antonyms: smooth, perfection.

Rhyme: ditch

"The Mars rover fell into the <u>ditch</u> and that caused the <u>glitch</u>."

gloss: (*glos*) noun, verb

the shine on a smooth surface; a superficially attractive appearance; a product that adds shine; an explanation of a word or phrase (n.)
to put gloss on something to make it shine; to provide an explanation (v.)

- The new products gave her hair a beautiful **gloss**.(n.)

- The car was **glossed** to make it look new. (v.)

Synonyms: glaze, shine, lustre, polish, sheen.

Antonyms: dullness, drabness.

Rhyme: floss

''He credits his dental gloss to a daily floss.''

gullible: (*guhl-uh-buhl*) adjective

easily fooled, deceived or cheated

- Tim had always been a rather naïve and **gullible** boy.

- As a child, she was so **gullible**, she would believe anything her sister told her.

Synonyms: naïve, credulous, innocent, trusting, foolish.

Antonyms: cynical, suspicious.

Rhyme: gull able

"The sea <u>gull</u> was <u>able</u> to fool the <u>gullible</u> fish by crying for help."

haughty: (*haw-tee*) adjective

arrogantly superior and disdainfully proud; full of oneself

- She addressed the staff in a **haughty**, superior tone.

- The new student gave me a **haughty** look as he walked away.

Synonyms: proud, arrogant, conceited, self-important.

Antonyms: shy, humble, meek, timid.

Rhyme: hot tea

''The <u>haughty</u> lady refused to drink the <u>hot tea</u> because it was not hot enough.''

headstrong: (*hed*-strawng) adjective

stubbornly wilful and determined to get one's way; refusing to change one's actions or opinions

- She is too **headstrong** to give up that easily.

- Sometimes, he can be so **headstrong** that it is impossible to reason with him.

Synonyms: impulsive, determined, wilful, stubborn, obstinate.

Antonyms: moderate, cautious, submissive, obedient, docile.

Rhyme: dead wrong

"She was <u>headstrong</u> even when she was <u>dead wrong</u>."

hierarchy: (*hahy*-*rahr*-*kee*) noun

a system that ranks people based on their status or authority;
an arrangement of things according to their relative importance

- Some animals have complex social **hierarchies**.

- She worked her way up to the top of the **hierarchy** at her company.

Synonyms: pecking order, ranking order, pyramid, echelon.

Antonyms: disorder, disarrangement, equality.

Rhyme: Monarchy

"The <u>Monarchy</u> had a very elaborate <u>hierarchy</u>."

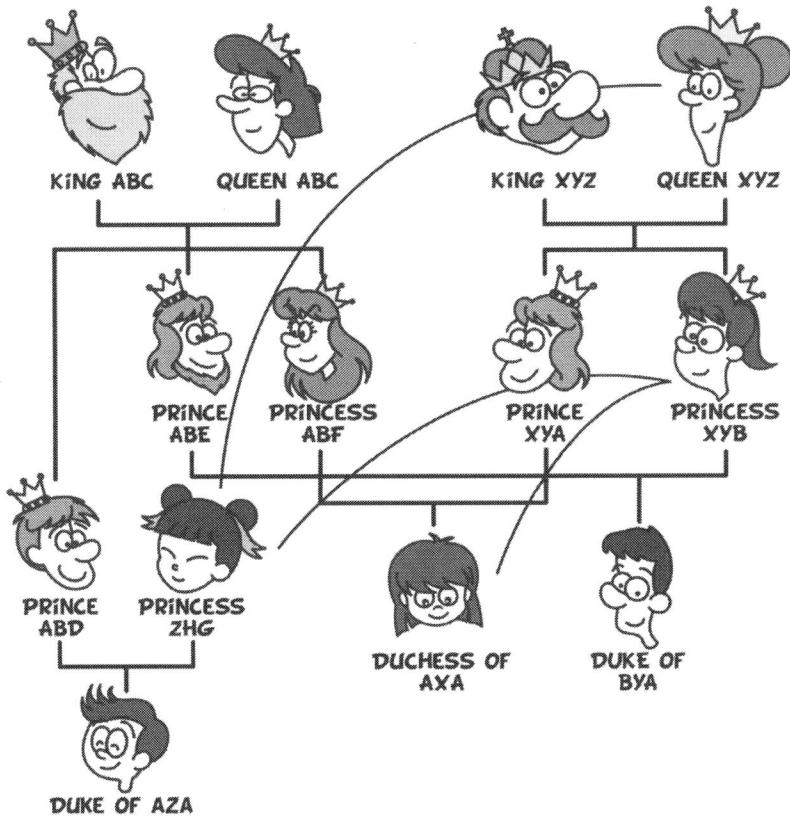

hoard: (*hawrd*) noun, verb

a stock of resources that is usually hidden or guarded (n.)
to accumulate resources and store them away; to keep in one's mind (v.)

- Some people like to share their knowledge, while others **hoard** it. (v.)

- They found a huge **hoard** of coins in his bedroom. (n.)

Synonyms: collection, stash, gather, store, hide away.

Antonyms: give, spend, share, hand out.

Rhyme: sword

"They found a <u>hoard</u> of ancient <u>swords</u> in their back garden."

hostile: (*hos-tl/ hos-tahyl*) adjective

feeling or showing dislike or opposition toward something or someone; unfriendly; belonging to a military enemy

- They have **hostile** feelings toward his family.

- Her **hostile** look indicated that she had no interest in talking to him.

Synonyms: aggressive, intimidating, unfriendly, antagonistic, harsh.

Antonyms: nice, kind, friendly, welcoming, agreeable.

Rhyme: host

"The <u>host</u> became <u>hostile</u> when I said I did not like the food!"

hypocrite: (*hip-uh-krit*) noun

someone who pretends to possess virtues, beliefs or morals that they do not actually have

- He is a **hypocrite** and only pretends to care about the needs of others.

- The media branded her a **hypocrite**, but she is one of the most honest people I have ever known.

Synonyms: charlatan, fraud, phony, impostor, pretender.

Antonyms: honest, truthful.

Rhyme: hippo cried

"The <u>hippo cried</u> when he accidentally killed an ant. What a <u>hypocrite</u>!"

hysterical: (*hi-ster-i-kuhl*) adjective

uncontrollably or irrationally emotional; incredibly funny

- Her anger and pain had made her **hysterical**.

- The comedy special was **hysterical**; I was laughing the entire time.

Synonyms: panicked, frenzied, frenetic, hilarious, uncontrollable.

Antonyms: calm, composed, collected, controlled, boring.

Rhyme: historical

"Reading about violent <u>historical</u> wars made him <u>hysterical</u>."

idiosyncrasy: (*id-ee-uh-**sin**-kruh-see*) noun

a habit, appearance or personality trait that is peculiar to an individual

- My neighbour's **idiosyncrasy** was that she always wore a pink hat wherever she went.

- We all have our own little **idiosyncrasies**.

Synonyms: peculiarity, eccentricity, mannerism, quirk, distinction.

Antonyms: commonality, normality, usualness.

Rhyme: idiot

"One of the King's idiosyncrasies was to play the village idiot in disguise."

imply: (*im-plahy*) verb

to hint at or suggest something without saying it openly; to signify or mean; to follow as a logical consequence

- Her tone of voice seemed to **imply** that she did agree with them.

- I did not mean to **imply** that you were lying.

Synonyms: suggest, hint, indicate, entail, involve.

Antonyms: state, define, express.

Rhyme: high

"The mountain was <u>high</u>, which <u>implied</u> they would need winter clothes."

incentive: (*in-**sen**-tiv*) noun

something, such as a reward, that motivates someone to act

- He needs an **incentive** to take on that project.

- The promise of a raise was a strong **incentive** for the workers that month.

Synonyms: motivation, reason, encouragement, stimulus, enticement.

Antonyms: block, prevention, hindrance, discouragement.

Rhyme: attentive

''The dogs became <u>attentive</u> when offered the right <u>incentive</u>.''

incongruous: (*in-**kong**-groo-uhs*) adjective

not in harmony with the surrounding objects or themes; out of place

- Even though their personalities seemed **incongruous**, they had a terrific relationship.

- These cars look **incongruous** in the middle of the historic town.

Synonyms: inconsistent, incompatible, inappropriate, contradictory, conflicting.

Antonyms: consistent, compatible, congruous, fitting, harmonious.

Rhyme: kangaroo in a bus

''The <u>kangaroo in a bus</u> seemed <u>incongruous</u>.''

indigenous: (*in-**dij**-uh-nuhs*) adjective

native to a particular place

- The botanist came to Australia to study their **indigenous** plants.
- The species of insects is **indigenous** to the Amazon rainforest.

Synonyms: native, local, aboriginal, home-grown, domestic.

Antonyms: foreign, alien.

Rhyme: indigestion

"The explorers got <u>indigestion</u> after eating the <u>indigenous</u> fruit."

inept: (*in-ept*) adjective

having no skill or aptitude for something; awkward or clumsy; absurd

- Despite his many other talents, Joseph was terribly **inept** at math.

- His failure left him feeling **inept**, but he vowed to keep trying until he succeeded.

Synonyms: incompetent, incapable, awkward, bumbling, absurd.

Antonyms: able, competent, capable, dexterous, skilful.

Rhyme: slept

"The soldier was <u>inept</u> and <u>slept</u> throughout the battle."

intrepid: (*in-trep-id*) adjective

fearless and adventurous

- She proved to be an **intrepid** leader on their voyage.

- He was an **intrepid** pioneer, always wanting to push the limits of what was possible and explore new options.

Synonyms: fearless, bold, courageous, heroic, audacious.

Antonyms: afraid, cowardly, fearful, timid, meek.

Rhyme: tripped

"The intrepid explorer tripped over a stone and became unconscious."

irate: (*ahy-reyt*) adjective

extremely angry

- In all these years, I had never seen my mother so **irate**.

- I sometimes enjoy reading **irate** comments on the internet to pass the time.

Synonyms: furious, enraged, fuming, livid, incensed.

Antonyms: calm, collected, tranquil, cool, unruffled.

Rhyme: I rate

"The customer was irate at the broken product and said 'I rate it zero' in frustration."

jeer: (*jeer*) noun, verb

a rude, mocking comment (n.)
to shout rude, mocking comments at someone (v.)

• Hearing the **jeers** and hisses of the audience was discouraging, but he managed to deliver his speech with great aplomb. (v.)

• His classmates shouted **jeers** at him in the hallway. (n.)

Synonyms: mock, boo, heckle, ridicule, taunt

Antonyms: cheer, applaud, compliment, praise, commend.

Rhyme: deer

''*The deer chased the lion* story was jeered at.''

jubilant: (*joo*-*buh*-*luhnt*) adjective

extremely happy and triumphant

- The children were **jubilant** to see their father again.

- The space crew was exhausted but **jubilant** when they returned to Earth.

Synonyms: joyous, thrilled, ecstatic, euphoric, triumphant.

Antonyms: depressed, discouraged, disappointed, unenthusiastic.

Rhyme: jumbo plant

''She was jubilant when her jumbo plant won the first prize.''

juvenile: (*joo-vuh-nahyl*) adjective, noun

intended for or relating to young people (adj.)
a young person (n.)

- The fifteen-year-old boy spent two months at a **juvenile** detention centre. (adj.)

- The **juvenile** was immature and had poor judgement. (n.)

Synonyms: young, childish, immature, adolescent, teenager.

Antonyms: old, mature, adult, experienced, grown-up.

Rhyme: jet's aisle

"During the long flight, the jet's aisle became a playground of the juvenile."

lacklustre: (*lak-luhs-ter*) adjective

lacking in brilliance, vitality or spirit; dull

- After a sleepless night of tossing and turning, I felt tired and **lacklustre**.

- The apartment looks **lacklustre** now but wait until I we start decorating!

Synonyms: boring, unimaginative, dull, uninspired, drab.

Antonyms: bright, lively, shiny, spirited, enthusiastic.

Rhyme: blockbuster

''The original movie was a <u>blockbuster</u>, but its sequel was <u>lacklustre</u>.''

languid: (*lang-**gwid***) adjective

relaxed and peaceful; lacking in vitality and vigour; weak from illness or fatigue

- She speaks in a quiet voice with a **languid** drawl.

- They went for a **languid** stroll through the gardens.

Synonyms: relaxed, leisurely, lazy, languorous, slow.

Antonyms: active, energetic, spirited, lively, animated.

Rhyme: language

''The illness made him feel <u>languid</u> and he started speaking in a strange <u>language</u>.''

lethargy: (*leth-er-jee*) noun

lack of energy or vitality; sluggish inactivity

- Extreme **lethargy** is one of the symptoms of his illness.

- After a hectic week at work, she was suddenly overcome by **lethargy**.

Synonyms: exhaustion, fatigue, laziness, sluggishness, lifelessness.

Antonyms: energy, stamina, liveliness, vigour, vitality.

Rhyme: <u>energy</u>

"The <u>lethargy</u> disappeared after he drank a bottle of super strong <u>energy</u> drink."

mercurial: (*mer-**kyoor**-ee-uhl*) adjective

subject to drastic and unpredictable changes in mood or behaviour; volatile; containing the element mercury

- It is a fickle and **mercurial** industry, only interested in making money.

- The painter's **mercurial** temperament allowed him to create breath-taking art but left him with almost no friends.

Synonyms: changeable, unpredictable, impulsive, volatile, fickle.

Antonyms: stable, constant, predictable, reliable, unchanging.

Rhyme: Mercury

"Planet <u>Mercury's</u> <u>mercurial</u> orbit surprised the Sun and other planets."

moat: (*moht*) noun

a deep, wide trench, usually filled with water, that surrounds a town or a castle to protect it

- The town was surrounded by an enormous **moat**.

- The soldier swam across the **moat** to rescue the King.

Synonyms: channel, canal, trench.

Antonyms: There are no antonyms for the word Moat.

Rhyme: boat

''The <u>moat</u> could only be crossed on a <u>boat</u>.''

morose: (*muh-rohs*) adjective

gloomy and ill-tempered

- He became quite **morose** when he heard the bad news.

- I have been feeling **morose** and irritable all morning and I don't know why.

Synonyms: miserable, glum, gloomy, sullen, melancholy.

Antonyms: bright, cheerful, light-hearted, optimistic, content.

Rhyme: my rose

"I was <u>morose</u> when <u>my</u> favourite <u>rose</u> died."

muddle: (*muhd-l*) noun, verb

a disorganized, messy state; a mistake caused by or resulting in confusion (n.)
to mix up, confuse or jumble; occupy oneself with aimless tasks (v.)

- Somehow, we found ourselves in a real **muddle**. (n.)

- The substitute teacher kept **muddling** everybody's names on the first day. (v.)

Synonyms: mess, disorder, confuse, jumble, disorganize.

Antonyms: order, clarity, neatness, organization, tidiness.

Rhyme: puddle

''The clear water became <u>muddled</u> when children jumped in the <u>puddle</u>.''

nuisance: (**nyoo**-suhns) noun

an inconvenient or annoying person, thing or condition

- Although we love our puppy, she can be a bit of **nuisance**.

- Forgetting your earphones at home is a terrible **nuisance**.

Synonyms: annoyance, pest, bother, irritant, trouble.

Antonyms: aid, help, convenience, comfort, pleasure.

Rhyme: new dance

''Neighbours' <u>new dance</u> practice was a <u>nuisance</u>.''

obdurate: (*ob-dyoo-rit*) adjective

stubbornly resistant to outside influence; unwilling to change one's mind

- She was **obdurate** in her moral convictions.

- Henry was the most **obdurate** student she had ever had.

Synonyms: stubborn, adamant, inflexible, heartless, unsympathetic.

Antonyms: compliant, submissive, yielding, gentle, susceptible.

Rhyme: moderate

"He tried to <u>moderate</u> but could not separate the <u>obdurate</u> debaters."

oscillate: (*os-uh-leyt*) verb

to swing back and forth in a regular manner; to go back and forth between two beliefs or opinions

- He **oscillated** between being friendly and arrogant.

- My older brother kept **oscillating** between staying and going.

Synonyms: hesitate, seesaw, waver, fluctuate, swing.

Antonyms: stabilize, decide.

Rhyme: overweight

"He seemed to <u>oscillate</u> between being <u>overweight</u> and underweight."

palatable: (*pal-uh-tuh-bul*) adjective

pleasant and acceptable, especially to the palate or taste; acceptable or satisfactory action or proposal

- The cake we ordered was barely **palatable**.

- The truth was not as **palatable** as the lies they were accustomed to hearing.

Synonyms: edible, acceptable, appetizing, agreeable, pleasant.

Antonyms: repulsive, unacceptable, unattractive, unpleasant.

Rhyme: plate and table

''The giant found the food so <u>palatable</u> that he ate the <u>plate and</u> the <u>table</u>.''

placate: (*pley*-keyt) verb

to make someone less anxious or angry; to appease someone's anger, usually by making concessions

- His reassuring words **placated** her anxiety.

- Instead of expressing herself authentically, she is trying to **placate** her biggest critics.

Synonyms: calm, soothe, pacify, appease, comfort.

Antonyms: enrage, annoy, agitate, aggravate, upset.

Rhyme: vacate

"The only way to placate the Martians was to vacate quickly!"

plight: (*plahyt*) noun

a difficult or unfortunate situation or state

- I am grateful that my friends sympathized with my **plight**.

- The **plight** of the homeless was near and dear to her heart.

Synonyms: predicament, difficulty, trouble, bind, situation, dilemma.

Antonyms: advantage, benefit, solution, fortune, blessing.

Rhyme: poor light

"Their <u>plight</u> was made worse by the <u>poor light</u>."

porous: (*pawr-uhs*) adjective

full of pores through which water and air can pass

- Her skin looked very **porous** after the sauna.

- If you place your plants in a **porous** container, you will have to water them frequently.

Synonyms: absorbent, leaky, spongy, permeable, penetrable.

Antonyms: impervious, impenetrable, nonporous, airtight.

Rhyme: poor us

"The rain fell through the <u>porous</u> roof, and they exclaimed '<u>poor us</u>!'"

portly: (*pawrt-lee*) adjective

having a heavy-set body; rather fat

- Our headmaster is a **portly** man with a friendly disposition.

- The **portly** young man was dressed in his finest suit.

Synonyms: overweight, stout, hefty, burly, well-built.

Antonyms: thin, skinny, slight, slim, slender.

Rhyme: sporty

"The <u>portly</u> man was surprisingly <u>sporty</u>."

potent: (*poht*-nt) adjective

powerful; producing powerful physical effects

- Large thrones used to be a **potent** symbol of authority.

- Charisma is a **potent** tool when it comes to public speaking.

Synonyms: strong, powerful, effective, compelling, mighty.

Antonyms: weak, ineffective, feeble, impotent, incapable.

Rhyme: pot

"The big <u>pot</u> was a <u>potent</u> ruler of all cutlery."

pragmatic: (*prag-**mat**-ik*) adjective

dealing with things realistically; basing decisions on practical rather than theoretical factors

- Our current situation requires a more **pragmatic** approach.

- He preferred to be idealistic instead of **pragmatic** in his worldview.

Synonyms: practical, realistic, down-to-earth, logical, hard-headed.

Antonyms: irrational, idealistic, unrealistic, impractical.

Rhyme: problematic

"The situation was <u>problematic</u>, and the only <u>pragmatic</u> thing was to climb up the tree."

precarious: (*pri-**kair**-ee-uhs*) adjective

not held in place securely; very likely to collapse; dependent on chance or other factors outside of one's control

- That old wooden staircase looks **precarious**.

- His employment status is **precarious** at the moment, and he doesn't know if there is anything he can do about it.

Synonyms: risky, dangerous, unstable, insecure, uncertain.

Antonyms: safe, certain, definite, reliable, secure.

Rhyme: curious

''I was <u>curious</u> and landed in a <u>precarious</u> position.''

prejudiced: (*prej-uh-dist*) adjective

having a preconceived negative feeling or opinion about something or someone

- The judges on the talent show were **prejudiced**, but the contestant managed to win them over.

- We were trying not to be **prejudiced** in the decision-making process.

Synonyms: biased, impartial, bigoted, narrow-minded, inclined.

Antonyms: unbiased, unprejudiced, fair, open-minded, receptive.

Rhyme: juiced

"He had a <u>prejudice</u> against <u>juiced</u> drinks and always ate raw fruits."

privation: (*prahy-**vey**-shun*) noun

a lack of the resources, bare necessities and comforts needed for one's well-being

- The two of them lived in a state of **privation** for years.

- Self-discipline is a form of voluntary **privation**.

Synonyms: hardship, deprivation, adversity, poverty, destitution.

Antonyms: abundance, luxury, plenty, wealth.

Rhyme: private tuition

"Lots of <u>private tuitions</u> resulted in <u>privation</u> as the little boy could not play with friends."

proportion: (*pruh-**pawr**-shunh*) noun, verb

a part viewed in relation to the other parts or the whole in terms of size; in comparison with; relative to (n.)
to adjust a part so that it is in harmony with the other parts or the whole (v.)

- The court decided to **proportion** the punishment to the crime. (v.)

- A large **proportion** of the population is single. (n.)

Synonyms: ration, part, share, quantity, dimension.

Antonyms: entirety, whole, imbalance, unevenness, disproportion.

Rhyme: portion

"Each child was given a <u>portion</u> in <u>proportion</u> to their height."

prowess: (*prou-is*) noun

exceptional expertise or skill in a field; great courage, especially in battle

- We were all in awe of her **prowess** as a hunter.

- His analytical **prowess** was often underestimated because of his friendly disposition.

Synonyms: ability, aptitude, proficiency, bravery, valour.

Antonyms: inability, incompetence, ineptitude, cowardice, weakness.

Rhyme: proudest

"His parents were the <u>proudest</u> when he was awarded for his <u>prowess</u> as an athlete."

qualm: (*kwahm*) noun

a feeling of worry, doubt or fear about one's conduct

- Despite my initial **qualms**, I knew I had chosen the best course of action.

- The new executive had no **qualms** about firing employees who were underperforming.

Synonyms: doubt, uneasiness, apprehension, scruple, remorse.

Antonyms: certainty, confidence, trust, sureness, assuredness.

Rhyme: calm

''He had no <u>qualms</u> about cheating and was <u>calm</u> when caught.''

quandary: (*kwon-duh-ree*) noun

a state of uncertainty about what to do; a dilemma

- Her insightful article thoroughly examines this **quandary**.

- My best friend helped me talk through my moral **quandary** and find the best solution.

Synonyms: dilomma, predicament, difficulty, plight, impasse.

Antonyms: solution, advantage, fortune.

Rhyme: laundry

"The broken machines at the <u>laundry</u> left him in a <u>quandary</u>."

rash: (*rash*) adjective, noun

acting too hastily without carefully considering the consequences (adj.)

an area of redness and itchy spots on one's skin, often due to an allergy (n.)

- It is best not to be **rash** when making major decisions that will impact the well-being of many people. (adj.)

- She discovered a strange **rash** on her forearms after picking herbs in the forest. (n.)

Synonyms: hasty, impulsive, reckless, imprudent, outbreak.

Antonyms: careful, cautious, sensible, prudent, timid.

Rhyme: crash

"His <u>rash</u> driving caused the <u>crash</u>."

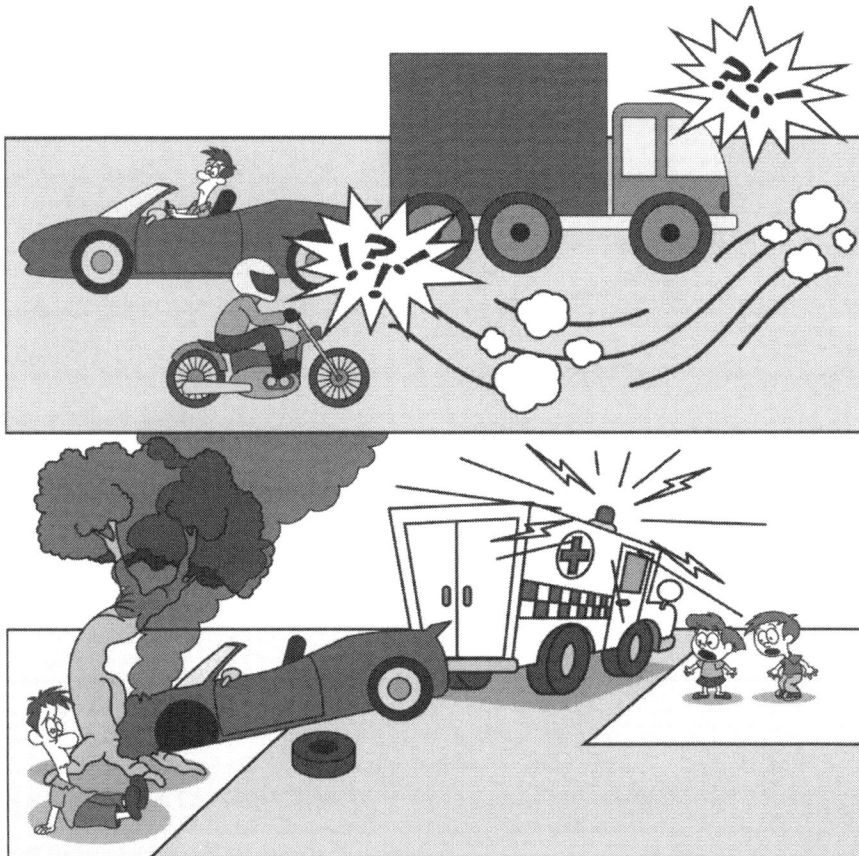

ratify: (*rat-uh-fahy*) verb

give formal consent to something, making it officially valid

- Many countries have yet to **ratify** the treaty.

- Once the protocol is **ratified**, we can start to implement the changes.

Synonyms: approve, sanction, authorise, confirm, accept.

Antonyms: reject, decline, refuse, disallow, deny.

Rhyme: rat

"The rat kings ratified the treaty."

raze: (*reyz*) verb

to tear down or demolish; to completely destroy

- The public protested against their plans to **raze** the park and replace it with a shopping mall.

- My neighbours **razed** their old house and rebuilt it from scratch.

Synonyms: destroy, demolish, bulldoze, annihilate, obliterate.

Antonyms: build, construct, create, repair, restore.

Rhyme: race

"The elephant <u>race</u> resulted in village huts being <u>razed</u> to the ground."

refute: (*ri-fyoot*) verb

to prove a statement or theory false; to deny or contradict an accusation or statement

- He was quick to **refute** any insult to his character.

- Their points were almost too easy to **refute** with facts.

Synonyms: disprove, contest, counter, negate, contradict.

Antonyms: prove, approve, concur, concede, confirm.

Rhyme: parachute

''The allegation that the <u>parachute</u> was faulty was difficult to <u>refute</u>.''

relinquish: (*ri-ling-kwish*) verb

to give up or release; to surrender

- The committee managed to convince him to **relinquish** his role to someone more capable.

- The leader of the country had no intention to **relinquish** his power.

Synonyms: surrender, abandon, resign, renounce, give up.

Antonyms: retain, allow, assert, continue, keep, maintain.

Rhyme: relish fish

"He relished eating fish but relinquished it after he became vegan."

reminisce: (*rem-uh-**nis***) verb

to recall the past

- My grandmother often **reminisces** about the adventures of her youth.

- The old actor was **reminiscing** about the first time he went to see a play as a little boy.

Synonyms: recall, evoke, remember, ruminate, recollect.

Antonyms: forget, ignore, neglect.

Rhyme: miss

"He <u>missed</u> his glory days and <u>reminisced</u> about them all day long."

renounce: (*ri-nouns*) verb

to formally reject or abandon something, such as a title, a cause or a claim

- The valiant knight shocked everyone by **renouncing** his loyalties to a corrupt lord.

- After months of fruitless effort, she decided to **renounce** the cause.

Synonyms: reject, relinquish, resign, discard, disown.

Antonyms: accept, embrace, allow, adopt, admit.

Rhyme: announce

''The bully <u>announced</u> that he was <u>renouncing</u> violence.''

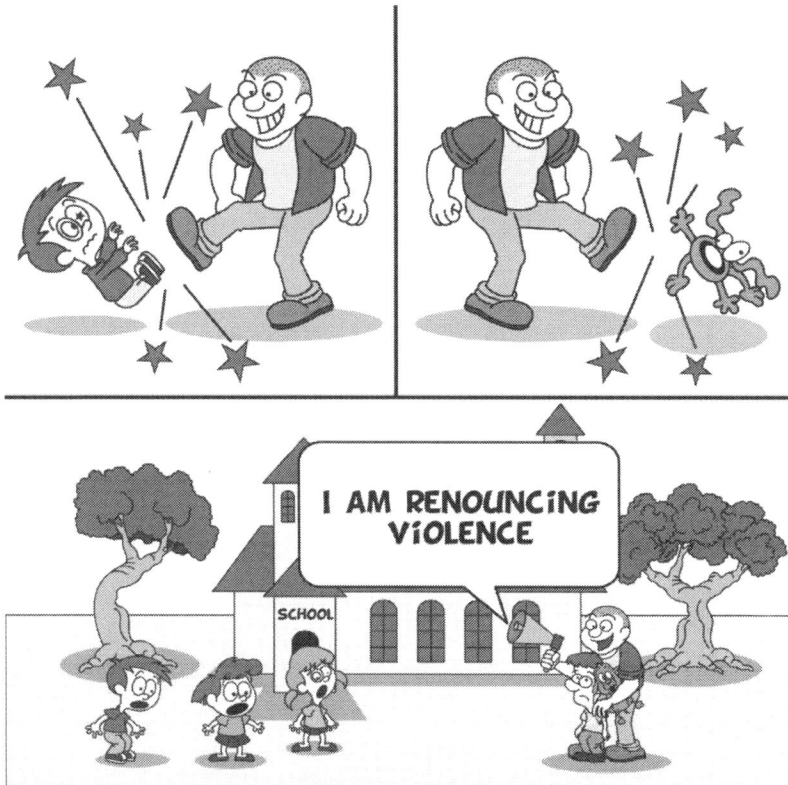

rue: (*roo*) verb

to bitterly regret one's actions

- She knew that one day, she would **rue** letting such an opportunity slip thorough her fingers.

- The criminal announced that they would **rue** the day they crossed his path.

Synonyms: regret, lament, grieve, deplore.

Antonyms: praise, apathy, delight.

Rhyme: zoo

"I <u>rue</u> the day I booed at the <u>zoo</u>."

ruthless: (*rooth-lis*) adjective

showing no pity, compassion or mercy

- Despite her small frame, she proved to be a **ruthless** competitor.

- The dictator was **ruthless** with anyone who dared to defy him.

Synonyms: cruel, callous, brutal, merciless, heartless.

Antonyms: merciful, civilized, forgiving, gentle, humane.

Rhyme: toothless

"The toothless king was ruthless."

salvage: (*sal-vij*) verb

to rescue a wrecked ship or its cargo from the sea; to retrieve something from adverse circumstances

- The divers managed to **salvage** the remnants of the ship from the ocean.

- He was working hard to **salvage** his reputation after the scandal.

Synonyms: save, recover, rescue, retrieve, restore, redeem.

Antonyms: abandon, forfeit, harm, injure, endanger.

Rhyme: savage

"They managed to <u>salvage</u> the boat after it was attacked by <u>savages</u>."

scrupulous: (*skroo-pyuh-luhs*) adjective

having or demonstrating a strong desire to behave morally; careful and very attentive to details

- The accountant was always **scrupulous** in his work.

- That woman is not as **scrupulous** as she purports to be.

Synonyms: conscientious, meticulous, honest, trustworthy.

Antonyms: careless, easy-going, dishonest, lenient, uncritical.

Rhyme: screw plus

"The screws with the plus sign had to be scrupulously bolted to make the old radio work."

seethe: (*seeth*) verb

to be bubbling and boiling; to be filled with anger that one is not expressing; to be crowded with people who are moving around quickly

- The water was **seething** on the stove.

- He was **seething** as he watched his competitor receive the award he wanted.

Synonyms: bubble, boil, fume, rage, swarm, buzz.

Antonyms: calm, freeze, relax.

Rhyme: breathe

"He was <u>seething</u> with anger and had to be helped to <u>breathe</u>."

sentry: (*sen-tree*) noun

a soldier stationed to keep watch over a place; a member of the guard

- The **sentry** defended the fortress against the invaders.

- I was on **sentry** duty at the gate yesterday.

Synonyms: guard, patrol, lookout, watch, sentinel.

Antonyms: There are no antonyms for the word Sentry.

Rhyme: entry

"To get an <u>entry</u>, you had to go past the <u>sentry</u>."

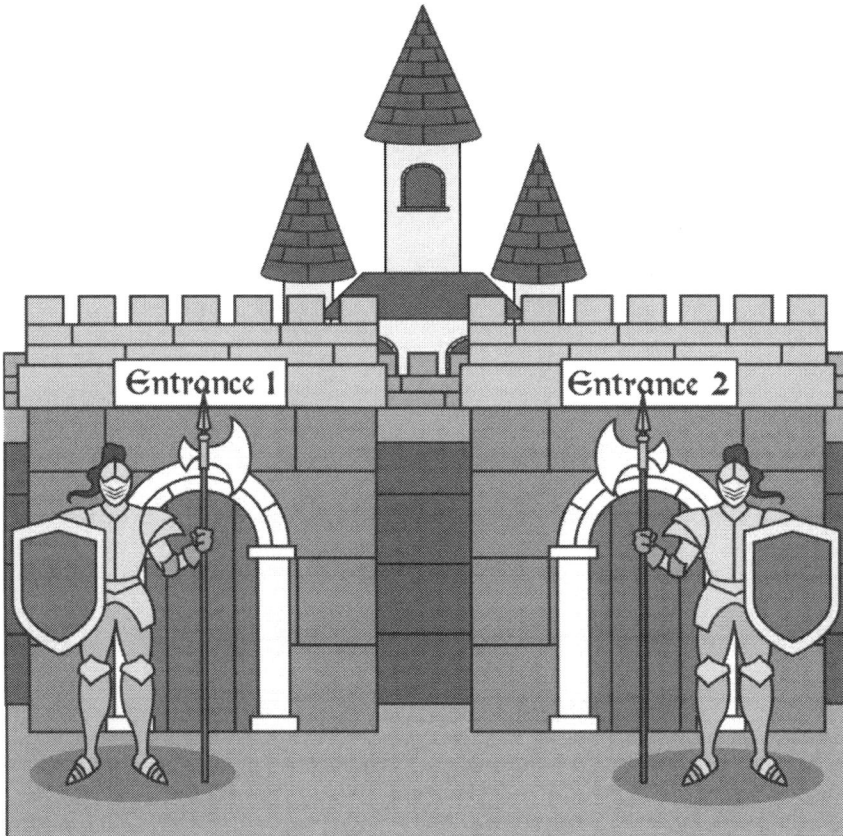

sham: (*sham*) adjective, noun, verb

false; fake (adj.)
a fraud or hoax; a person who pretends to be something they are not (n.)
to pretend; to present something false as the truth (v.)

- The dictator held **sham** elections to fool the citizens. (adj.)

- The statistics they presented were a **sham**. (n.)

Synonyms: fake, bogus, pretence, deception.

Antonyms: real, authentic, genuine, sincere.

Rhyme: shampoo

''The shampoo was clearly a sham.''

sinister: (*sin-uh-ster*) adjective

criminal, evil or wicked; seeming to indicate that something evil or harmful is going to happen

- The dark, empty room had a **sinister** appearance.

- Something tells me his plans are more **sinister** than he lets on.

Synonyms: evil, ominous, threatening, disturbing, malevolent.

Antonyms: good, lucky, nice, kind, benevolent.

Rhyme: little sister

''For some reason they thought that her <u>little sister</u> was <u>sinister</u>.''

sly: (*slahy*) adjective

cunning and deceitful; hinting that one has secret knowledge about something

- Diana is a clever but **sly** woman.

- The young man gave us a **sly** smile as we left the room.

Synonyms: cunning, crafty, artful, devious, underhand.

Antonyms: naïve, foolish, simple, honest, straightforward.

Rhyme: lie

"The <u>sly</u> wolf <u>lied</u> to little Red Riding Hood."

sparse: (*spahrs*) adjective

thinly scattered or distributed over an area; scarce

- The man's thick hair had become thin and **sparse**.

- The available information on that topic is **sparse**.

Synonyms: infrequent, scarce, spare, thin, dispersed.

Antonyms: dense, abundant, frequent, full, plentiful.

Rhyme: farce

"The audience were <u>sparse</u> because the show was a <u>farce</u>."

splinter: (*splin-ter*) noun, verb

a small, thin and sharp piece of material broken off the main body (n.)
to break into splinters (v.)

- I used a pair of tweezers to get the **splinter** out of my finger. (n.)

- The glass cracked from the heat but did not **splinter**. (v.)

Synonyms: fragment, sliver, shard, disintegrate, shatter.

Antonyms: whole, repair, mend.

Rhyme: sprinter

"The ace sprinter was stopped by a splinter."

squabble: (*skwob-uhl*) noun, verb

a quarrel about something unimportant (n.)
to argue about something unimportant (v.)

- My neighbours are having their evening **squabble** as usual. (n.)

- His grandfather loves to **squabble** with us over meaningless matters. (v.)

Synonyms: quarrel, dispute, argument, argue, bicker.

Antonyms: reconciliation, agree, make peace.

Rhyme: square bubble

"There was a squabble over who would burst the square bubbles."

stampede: (*stam-**peed***) noun, verb

a sudden, frenzied rush of animals or a mass of people (n.)
to rush wildly in a mass frenzy (v.)

- That was the first time she had seen a real-life cattle **stampede**.

- The children **stampeded** through the small garden, playing tag.

Synonyms: charge, rush, pandemonium, hurry, dash.

Antonyms: retreat, linger, dally.

Rhyme: stamp paid

"Just as she had <u>paid</u> for the <u>stamps</u>, there was a <u>stampede</u> of people trying to run out of the post office due to fire."

stark: (*stahrk*) adjective

having a severe or bare appearance or outline; unpleasantly sharp; complete and utter

- We were standing in a **stark** white room that had no windows.

- Many thought that the daredevil was **stark** raving mad.

Synonyms: blunt, obvious, glaring, severe, absolute.

Antonyms: ambiguous, unnoticeable, subtle, lush, partial.

Rhyme: park

''With only one slide and trees without leaves the big <u>park</u> looked <u>stark</u>.''

steadfast: (*sted-fast*) adjective

firm and unchangeable, usually in purpose or resolution

- The coach's **steadfast** confidence in his team never wavered.

- She remained **steadfast** in her belief that changing careers was the right thing to do.

Synonyms: unwavoring, persistent, adamant, loyal, inflexible.

Antonyms: wavering, compliant, irresolute, flexible, disloyal.

Rhyme: study fast

"I had to be <u>steadfast</u> in <u>studying fast</u> for my approaching exams."

strive: (*strahyv*) verb

to try very hard to reach a goal

- He **strives** to be the best version of himself every day.

- I **strive** to make my life fulfilling and meaningful.

Synonyms: aim, endeavour, seek, attempt, try.

Antonyms: surrender, relax, discourage, yield, idle.

Rhyme: arrive

''The salmon <u>strived</u> hard and finally <u>arrived</u>.''

submerged: (*suhb-murjd*) adjective

gone or placed under the surface of water; completely covered or hidden

- The boy **submerged** the rubber duck in the bathwater.

- The architect was completely **submerged** in his sketches.

Synonyms: immersed, engulfed, flooded, swamped.

Antonyms: surfaced.

Rhyme: emerged

"Nobody guessed that there was a <u>submerged</u> sub till it suddenly <u>emerged</u>."

subside: (*suhb-sahyd*) verb

to become less intense; to become quiet or inactive; to sink and settle

- The storm outside has completely **subsided**.

- Her anger was starting to **subside**, so we decided to give her a little space.

Synonyms: recede, abate, ease up, relent, lessen.

Antonyms: intensify, worsen.

Rhyme: bedside

''His fever magically <u>subsides</u> when his pet turtle is by his <u>bedside</u>.''

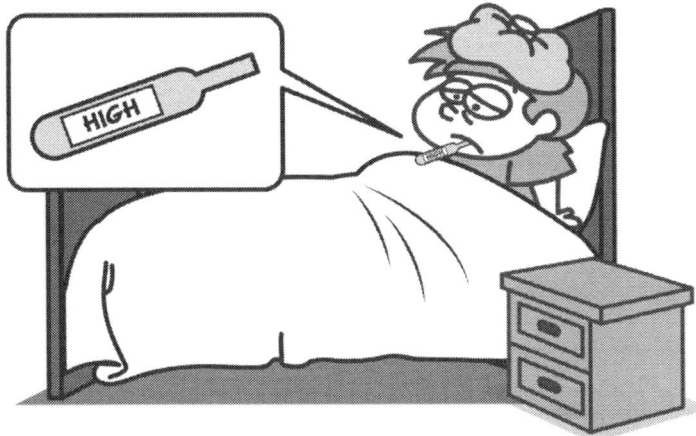

subterfuge: (*suhb-ter-fyooj*) noun

a lie or deceit used to achieve a goal

- I could see right through their **subterfuge**.

- No one would have ever suspected that her innocent demeanour hid a tremendous talent for **subterfuge**.

Synonyms: trick, deception, ruse, cheating, deceit.

Antonyms: honesty, openness.

Rhyme: huge

''He used <u>subterfuge</u> to make <u>huge</u> amounts of money.''

subterranean: (*suhb-tuh-**rey**-nee-uhn*) adjective

beneath the surface of the earth; underground; operating in secret

- The creature lived in a large, **subterranean** cavern.

- They were part of a **subterranean** effort to take over the world.

Synonyms: underground, concealed, sunken, secret, hidden.

Antonyms: aboveground, overhead, overt, open.

Rhyme: Pomeranian

"His Pomeranian dog loved digging subterranean tunnels to hide his bones."

succumb: (*suh-kuhm*) verb

to yield or give way to a superior force

- She refused to **succumb** to their influence.

- After hours of persuasion, he finally **succumbed** to her wishes.

Synonyms: surrender, yield, submit, give in.

Antonyms: resist, withstand, conquer.

Rhyme: suck thumb

''The baby finally <u>succumbed</u> to <u>sucking</u> his <u>thumb</u> even though he had mittens on.''

swarm: (*swawrm*) noun, verb

a big group of flying insects, people or things (n.)
to move together in a swarm (v.)

- A **swarm** of mosquitoes flew into the room when I opened the door. (n.)

- A large group of tourists was **swarming** around the streets, taking pictures. (v.)

Synonyms: flock, crowd, pack, flood.

Antonyms: disperse, scatter.

Rhyme: storm

"Even the storm could not deter the angry swarm."

thwart: (*thwart*) verb

to prevent from accomplishing a goal; to oppose successfully

- Her opponents tried hard to **thwart** her victory.

- We must **thwart** his schemes before it is too late!

Synonyms: impede, hinder, stop, prevent, foil.

Antonyms: support, endorse, expedite.

Rhyme: throw dart

"He thwarted the robber's plans by throwing darts."

toil: (*toil*) noun, verb

hard work (n.)
to work hard (v.)

- She dreams of a life free from unfulfilling **toil**. (n.)

- Talent is not enough to succeed; you also need to **toil**. (v.)

Synonyms: labour, work, effort, exertion.

Antonyms: rest, relax.

Rhyme: oil

''The result of their toil was lots of oil.''

tome: (*tohm*) noun

a large, heavy scholarly book; a volume of a series of works

- The prolific philosopher had written **tomes** about his beloved ideas.

- His bookshelves were lined with **tomes** on different interesting topics.

Synonyms: book, volume, work, publication.

Antonyms: There are no antonyms for the word Tome.

Rhyme: tomb

"They discovered the <u>tome</u> in the ancient <u>tomb</u>."

trench: (*trench*) noun

a long, narrow ditch or channel;
a long and narrow depression in the ocean bed

- The construction workers were digging a **trench** beside the road.

- The soldiers dug a **trench** in the ground.

Synonyms: ditch, channel, pit, rut, trough.

Antonyms: hill, hump, mound, rampart.

Rhyme: bench

''The strange park had <u>benches</u> in <u>trenches</u>.''

uniform: (*yoo-nuh-fawrm*) adjective, noun

having a similar form or character (adj.)
a distinctive outfit worn by members of the same organization or school (n.)

- The pattern on the wallpaper was made up of numerous **uniform** circles. (adj.)

- The students are required to wear a **uniform** to school. (n.)

Synonyms: constant, consistent, unvarying, costume, attire.

Antonyms: different, changeable, variable, varied.

Rhyme: inform

"All students were <u>informed</u> of the new <u>uniform</u>, but he missed the mail!"

unkempt: (*uhn-kempt*) adjective

messy or dishevelled; not cared for; neglected

- The old man's beard was knotted and **unkempt**.

- Everything about him was **unkempt**, from his clothing to his room.

Synonyms: untidy, messy, disordered, scruffy, dishevelled.

Antonyms: neat, tidy, orderly.

Rhyme: contempt

"He was <u>unkempt,</u> and the others treated him with <u>contempt</u>."

unpalatable: (*uhn-**pal**-uh-tuh-buhl*) adjective

having an unpleasant taste; unacceptable

- The meal they served us looked **unpalatable**, but it tasted quite good.

- Her extreme views are **unpalatable** to many listeners.

Synonyms: unappetizing, uninviting, unappealing, inedible.

Antonyms: palatable, inviting, delicious, appealing.

Rhyme: vegetable

''The <u>vegetable</u> cake was extremely <u>unpalatable</u>.''

usurp: (*yoo-surp*) verb

to take hold of power by force or deceit

- He wanted to **usurp** the principal's position.

- The king's son was falsely accused of wanting to **usurp** his father's throne.

Synonyms: seize, take, appropriate, steal, take over.

Antonyms: alleviate, appease, calm, delight, improve.

Rhyme: slurp

''While the young prince was busy <u>slurping</u>, his kingdom was <u>usurped</u>.''

vandalize: (*van-dl-ahyz*) verb

to deface or destroy

- It is forbidden to **vandalize** public property.

- Our neighbour's car had been **vandalized** with spray paint.

Synonyms: deface, sabotage, wreck, ruin.

Antonyms: clumsy, inactive, slow, sluggish.

Rhyme: scandalize

''The whole town was <u>scandalized</u> when the statue of the local hero was <u>vandalized</u>.''

verbose: (*ver-bohs*) adjective

using too many words when speaking or writing

- His writing is always long and **verbose**.

- My best friend is a notoriously **verbose** speaker.

Synonyms: wordy, loquacious, talkative.

Antonyms: reticent, succinct, laconic.

Rhyme: verbal overdose

"The after-dinner speaker was <u>verbose,</u> and some people collapsed at the <u>verbal overdose</u>."

verve: (*vurv*) noun

vigour or enthusiasm; liveliness

- The comedian told his jokes with remarkable **verve** and wit.

- The children ran around the playground with **verve** and excitement.

Synonyms: enthusiasm, vigour, energy, vitality, vivacity.

Antonyms: lethargy, reluctance, apathy.

Rhyme: serve

''Although he was old, his <u>serve</u> had <u>verve</u>.''

vex: (*veks*) verb

to irritate or annoy, usually over trivial things

- What **vexed** me the most was their unwillingness to cooperate.
- My mother was **vexed** with me for not cleaning my room.

Synonyms: annoy, irritate, irk, infuriate, anger.

Antonyms: appease, mollify.

Rhyme: T-Rex

"The mighty T-Rex was vexed by the tiny bees."

vigorous: (*vig-er-uhs*) adjective

strong, healthy and energetic; forceful; requiring effort, strength and energy

- Before going to space, astronauts must complete a **vigorous** training program.

- He remained lively and **vigorous** well into his old age.

Synonyms: enthusiastic, brisk, spirited, forceful, robust.

Antonyms: frail, weak, light.

Rhyme: wig

"When his exercise became <u>vigorous</u>, his <u>wig</u> quickly came off!"

volatile: (***vol**-uh-til/ **vol**-uh-tahyl*) adjective

changing suddenly and unpredictably; subject to quick and unpredictable changes of emotion; evaporating quickly

- Jeremy's **volatile** nature often took people by surprise.

- Prices have been **volatile** all year.

Synonyms: unstable, unpredictable, explosive, precarious.

Antonyms: stable, predictable.

Rhyme: wet tiles

"Wet tiles on the dance floor meant that the party was going to be volatile."

voluble: (***vol****-yuh-buhl*) adjective

speaking fluently; speaking continuously without break

- She is a charming and **voluble** woman who always tells engaging stories.

- Although he was normally a **voluble** conversationalist, he was at a loss for words.

Synonyms: talkative, chatty, verbose, garrulous, loquacious.

Antonyms: reticent, taciturn, quiet.

Rhyme: volume up

''My friend is so <u>voluble</u> that when he is around, I turn the <u>volume up</u>.''

voyage: (*voi*-*ij*) noun, verb

a long journey (n.)
to travel or go on a long journey (v.)

- The explorers embarked on a **voyage** across the ocean. (n.)

- She spent the summer **voyaging** around Europe. (v.)

Synonyms: journey, expedition, travel, trip, trek.

Antonyms: stay.

Rhyme: boy age

''The interstellar <u>voyage</u> was so long that the <u>boy aged</u> by end of
it.''

wither: (*with-er*) verb

to fade, shrivel and decay; to decline or weaken; to lose the vigour of youth

- The roses that were once so vibrant had **withered** because of the heat.

- Good ideas will **wither** away if we do not act on them.

Synonyms: shrivel, wane, fade, wilt, droop.

Antonyms: thrive, grow, strengthen, flourish.

Rhyme: weather

"The harsh <u>weather</u> caused the plants to <u>wither</u>."

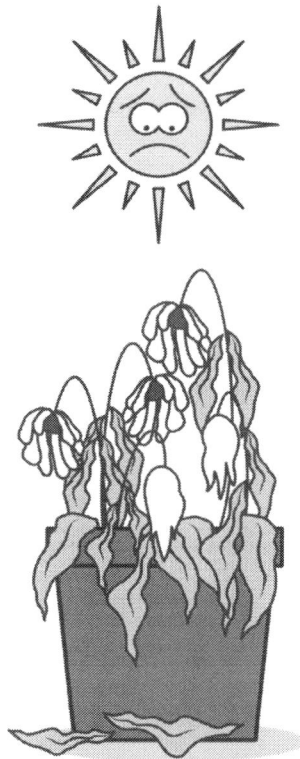

wrath: (*rath*) noun

fierce anger or vengeance

- She feared her employer's **wrath**.

- We were fortunate to escape the king's **wrath**.

Synonyms: fury, rage, anger, ire, madness.

Antonyms: happiness, calmness, peace.

Rhyme: math

''He faced the teachers' <u>wrath</u> when he could not do simple <u>math</u>.''

Review Exercises

Review Exercise 1

Match the word with its definition.

___ 1. **abduct**   a. physically or mentally quick and nimble
___ 2. **accentuate**   b. to make something seem big more impressive
___ 3. **acclaim**   c. to take away by force
___ 4. **accord**   d. to make worse
___ 5. **acumen**   e. public praise
___ 6. **adamant**   f. agreement, concurrence or harmony of things
___ 7. **adorn**   g. the ability to make good judgements
___ 8. **aggrandize**   h. to decorate
___ 9. **aggravate**   i. not willing to change one's mind
___10. **agile**   j. to make more noticeable and prominent

From the words above, fill in the blanks with the most appropriate word. (You may need to change the word form)

1. She wore a pink scarf that _____ her skin tone.

2. The salesman did not have the business _____ to close the deal.

3. The little girl's hair was_____ with flowers.

4. Using force to quell the protests will only_____ the situation.

5. I am glad that your ideas are in _____ with mine.

6. The new manager sought to _____ himself in front of his colleagues.

7. She was _____ about going to work even though she didn't feel well.

8. The scientist earned _____ for his ground-breaking research.

9. The debater had a quick and _____ mind that allowed him to think of impressive arguments on the spot.

10. The kidnappers tried to _____ the heiress but their plans were thwarted by the police.

Review Exercise 2

Match the word with its definition.

___ 1. **aloof** a. the highest point
___ 2. **amass** b. full of energy, life or spirit
___ 3. **ambiguous** c. something that is different from what is normal
___ 4. **amble** d. having several meanings or interpretations
___ 5. **anguish** e. to utterly destroy or defeat
___ 6. **animated** f. extreme pain or suffering
___ 7. **annihilate** g. to gather together
___ 8. **annul** h. a leisurely walk
___ 9. **anomaly** i. cool and reserved
___10. **apex** j. to revoke the legal status

From the words above, fill in the blanks with the most appropriate word. (You may need to change the word form)

1. The author has _____ a great fortune thanks to her bestselling trilogy.

2. The doctor's role in the mystery remains _____.

3. The singer left the music industry just as she reached the _____ of her career.

4. I love to _____ in the park in the evenings.

5. The contract was_____ because one of the parties had been dishonest.

6. The _____ was clear in her face as she told us her sad story.

7. The little boy's enthusiasm _____ everyone in the room.

8. Our hockey team _____ the visiting team in last night's game.

9. The speaker came across as _____ and unfriendly in his speech.

10. Astronomers still cannot explain the _____ they detected in the sky.

Review Exercise 3

Match the word with its definition.

___ 1. **aplomb**   a. to attack or criticise
___ 2. **applause**   b. clothing, usually for formal events
___ 3. **arduous**   c. to surprise
___ 4. **assail**   d. to gather into one place or unit
___ 5. **assemble**   e. having keen judgement
___ 6. **astonish**   f. loud enough to be heard
___ 7. **astute**   g. requiring great effort and exertion
___ 8. **atone**   h. showing approval or praise by clapping
___ 9. **attire**   i. unshakeable self-assurance
___10. **audible**   j. to make amends for one's offenses or mistakes

From the words above, fill in the blanks with the most appropriate word. (You may need to change the word form)

1. John spoke to the aggressive journalist with _____.

2. Although the hike was _____ the view from the top of the mountain was worth it.

3. We forgave him after he _____ for his offenses.

4. At the end of the lecture, the audience bust into _____.

5. Her mind was _____ by doubts about the decision she had to make the next morning.

6. We were told to dress in formal _____ for the reception.

7. I need some time to _____ my thoughts before I write this essay.

8. My mother is an _____ judge of character.

9. Even though the actors did not have microphones, their voices were still _____ in the back row.

10. We were _____ by the petite opera singer's powerful voice.

Review Exercise 4

Match the word with its definition.

___ 1. **banquet**   a. to make something dirty
___ 2. **barrage**   b. a lavish formal meal for many guests
___ 3. **bask**   c. a prejudice toward or against a person or a group
___ 4. **bastion**   d. to lie in the warm light for pleasure and relaxation
___ 5. **bedraggled**   e. artillery fire used to cover a military advance
___ 6. **benefactor**   f. expressing kindness and goodwill
___ 7. **benevolent**   g. having no harmful effects
___ 8. **benign**   h. something or someone that upholds principles
___ 9. **besmirch**   i. someone who invests money in a cause
___10. **bias**   j. having a dishevelled appearance

From the words above, fill in the blanks with the most appropriate word. (You may need to change the word form)

1. The charity received a large sum of money from an unknown
    _____.

2. He was completely _____ when he came home during the storm.

3. The _____ young man held the door open for the old woman.

4. The doctor informed us that the tumour was _____.

5. The carefully orchestrated _____ allowed them to win the battle.

6. The media tried to _____ her reputation but failed because she was far too clever for them.

7. Her birthday dinner looked more like a royal _____.

8. The ancient statue still stands as a _____ of growth and resilience.

9. The young author was _____ in the glory of his first book.

10. She assured us that her final decision would be free from _____.

Review Exercise 5

Match the word with its definition.

___ 1. **blandishment** a. a hiding place, usually in the ground
___ 2. **blemish** b. a state of supreme joy
___ 3. **bliss** c. to criticise someone severely
___ 4. **bounty** d. a small flaw
___ 5. **brazen** e. a break or a rupture
___ 6. **breach** f. flattery used to persuade someone
___ 7. **cache** g. to surrender
___ 8. **callous** h. lacking in sympathy for others
___ 9. **capitulate** i. bold and shameless
___10. **castigate** j. generosity in giving

From the words above, fill in the blanks with the most appropriate word. (You may need to change the word form)

1. His _____comments about the tragedy spoiled the mood for us.

2. The powerful leader was used to adulation and _____.

3. The soldiers could not resist any longer, so they_____ to the enemy forces.

4. The outspoken woman had a _____ disregard for authority.

5. Thanks to his healthy lifestyle, there was not a single _____ on his glowing skin.

6. The young woman found it difficult to forgive such an appalling _____ of her trust.

7. After the successful premiere the performers were in a state of pure_____.

8. Do not _____ them before listening to their side of the story.

9. The squirrels in our backyard have compiled an impressive _____ of nuts for the cold winter months.

10. Our local farmer's market offers the very best of nature's incredible _____.

Review Exercise 6

Match the word with its definition.

__ 1. **catapult**	a. the act of empathizing with someone's pain
__ 2. **cease**	b. an ornate light that hangs from the ceiling
__ 3. **celerity**	c. extremely large
__ 4. **chandelier**	d. to stop
__ 5. **chaos**	e. a device used to hurl or launch an object
__ 6. **clemency**	f. an act of forgiveness or mercy
__ 7. **collude**	g. uncritical self-satisfaction
__ 8. **colossal**	h. speed or swiftness of movement
__ 9. **commiseration**	i. a state of complete disorder
__10. **complacent**	j. to work together in secret

From the words above, fill in the blanks with the most appropriate word. (You may need to change the word form)

1. They used a _____ to launch the aircraft from the deck of the ship.

2. After losing his job, the man's life was plunged into utter _____.

3. He could only offer her his love and _____ in her time of need.

4. What are we going to do about this _____ failure?

5. The employee was accused of _____ with the company's biggest competitor.

6. I bought the most beautiful _____ for my dining room.

7. The law was passed with _____ due to the huge public outcry.

8. She demanded that he _____ all communications with her because she no longer wanted to see him.

9. Unfortunately, the court could not grant him _____.

10. Because the writers had grown _____ over the years, the quality of the show really deteriorated.

Review Exercise 7

Match the word with its definition.

___ 1. **concave**   a. act of helping two parties resolve a dispute
___ 2. **conciliation**   b. curved inwards
___ 3. **concur**   c. seeming challenging to overcome
___ 4. **confound**   d. to feel or express strong disapproval
___ 5. **conjecture**   e. permission or approval
___ 6. **consent**   f. a sudden and often humiliating failure
___ 7. **conundrum**   g. to confuse or surprise someone
___ 8. **daunting**   h. something that confuses
___ 9. **debacle**   i. an opinion formed on incomplete evidence
___10. **deplore**   j. to agree in opinion

From the words above, fill in the blanks with the most appropriate word. (You may need to change the word form)

1. We had her _____ to use her song in our short film.

2. We absolutely _____ all forms of violence.

3. The sudden spike in infections without apparent cause_____ the experts.

4. I have taken on the _____ task of writing my first novel.

5. Most of the arguments she presented in her article were based on pure _____ and had no basis in reality.

6. Our views on company policy do not _____.

7. She was very pleased with her new _____ lenses that corrected her vision.

8. After last night's _____, he wasn't sure how could show his face at the boxing club ever again.

9. My parents were in a bit of a _____ when they missed their connecting flight.

10. Relations between the two parties improved significantly after the successful _____.

Review Exercise 8

Match the word with its definition.

__	1. **deride**	a.	unconventional or a little strange
__	2. **detest**	b.	to ridicule, mock or express contempt for
__	3. **dexterous**	c.	sorrowful, mournful or melancholy
__	4. **disconnected**	d.	to wet or soak fully
__	5. **dogma**	e.	to feel strong dislike for something
__	6. **dogmatic**	f.	demonstrating skill, especially with one's hands
__	7. **doleful**	g.	asserting certain beliefs as unquestionably true
__	8. **domicile**	h.	principles proclaimed to be indisputably true
__	9. **drench**	i.	legal place of residence
__	10. **eccentric**	j.	having a poor or broken connection

From the words above, fill in the blanks with the most appropriate word. (You may need to change the word form)

1. He fell into the canal and was_____ .

2. She proved to be quite _____ at knitting intricate patterns.

3. The party's political _____ did not resonate with my core values.

4. His new position requires frequent changes in _____, so he will get to live in different countries.

5. Her colourful apartment filled with objects from all over the world suited her _____ personality perfectly.

6. The street musician filled the air with the _____ strains of his violin that made me feel sad.

7. I _____ people who don't treat others with basic respect.

8. Classical music fans often tend to _____ popular songs.

9. I was feeling _____ from nature, so last weekend, I went on a long hike in the mountains.

10. The athlete was almost _____ in his belief in the virtues of self-discipline.

Review Exercise 9

Match the word with its definition.

__ 1. **ecstatic**   a. rude or shameless boldness
__ 2. **edict**   b. to protect data by converting into code
__ 3. **eerie**   c. an official decree or proclamation
__ 4. **effrontery**   d. strange and scary
__ 5. **egregious**   e. extremely thin
__ 6. **elated**   f. to imitate in order to equal or surpass
__ 7. **elation**   g. extremely bad or shocking
__ 8. **emaciated**   h. a feeling of great joy or pride
__ 9. **emulate**   i. incredibly happy or proud
__ 10. **encrypt**   j. feeling extreme joy

From the words above, fill in the blanks with the most appropriate word. (You may need to change the word form)

1. The little boy wanted to _____ his favourite superheroes.

2. He is overweight now, but looks completely _____ in those old photos.

3. Getting involved in their private affairs was an_____ mistake.

4. My mood kept alternating between despair and _____.

5. He had the _____ to ask for more money, even though he hadn't paid her back yet.

6. The _____ music in the haunted house sent a shiver down my spine.

7. _____ fans rushed to the court after their team won the championship.

8. You can use this tool to _____ your confidential files.

9. I was _____ when I received the acceptance letter from the prestigious university.

10. We did not agree with the changes that the new _____ would entail.

Review Exercise 10

Match the word with its definition.

__	1. **encumber**	a.	extremely happy or excited
__	2. **endeavour**	b.	attempt
__	3. **endorse**	c.	respect and admiration
__	4. **enhance**	d.	to gradually wear away
__	5. **enigmatic**	e.	fair and equal
__	6. **equitable**	f.	mysterious
__	7. **erode**	g.	to avoid or escape by using deceit and trickery
__	8. **esteem**	h.	to publicly declare approval or support of
__	9. **euphoric**	i.	to block or impede the free movement of
__	10. **evade**	j.	to improve the quality of

From the words above, fill in the blanks with the most appropriate word. (You may need to change the word form)

1. The learned professor was held in_____ by the students.

2. His obsession with becoming rich and famous _____ with time.

3. The thief managed to_____ the police.

4. I will _____ to help you improve your grades, but cannot guarantee anything.

5. Each of you will receive an _____ cut of the total earnings.

6. A healthy diet, exercise and good sleep can help you _____ your athletic performance.

7. Not only were her new clothes extremely uncomfortable, but they also _____ her movement.

8. The painter was fascinated by her_____ beauty.

9. They refused to _____ the committee's outrageous views.

10. I was _____ when I found out that I had won the lottery.

Review Exercise 11

Match the word with its definition.

___	1. **exalted**	a. high in status or rank
___	2. **exasperated**	b. frequently changing one's affections and loyalties
___	3. **expel**	c. inactive or unproductive
___	4. **exult**	d. a formal oath of loyalty
___	5. **fallow**	e. extremely concerned with detail and cleanliness
___	6. **fastidious**	f. showing exaggerated flattery or affection
___	7. **fawning**	g. a remarkable act or accomplishment
___	8. **fealty**	h. to remove someone from an organization
___	9. **feat**	i. to feel or express triumphant joy and elation
___	10. **fickle**	j. extremely irritated or frustrated

From the words above, fill in the blanks with the most appropriate word. (You may need to change the word form)

1. They tried to _____ her from the organization but lacked sufficient proof of misconduct.

2. He _____ when he won the jackpot.

3. He is overly _____ about his dietary habits and always eats home cooked food.

4. I was _____ by his incessant complaints.

5. The young men demonstrated their dedication to their leader by swearing _____ to him.

6. Whenever the CEO entered the room, the employees became _____ and servile because they wanted to impress her.

7. Her_____ position gives her a great deal of influence over the Corporation.

8. Running a successful business is an impressive _____.

9. Few people could put up with his _____ personality.

10. The band went through a long _____ period in which they were not producing any music.

Review Exercise 12

Match the word with its definition.

__ 1.	**fidget**	a.	the shine on a smooth surface
__ 2.	**flaccid**	b.	a defect, error or malfunction
__ 3.	**flaunt**	c.	great delight or pleasure
__ 4.	**flout**	d.	to stare with one's mouth wide open
__ 5.	**forthright**	e.	a state or period of wild excitement or behaviour
__ 6.	**frenzy**	f.	frank and outspoken
__ 7.	**gape**	g.	openly disregard
__ 8.	**glee**	h.	to display something or someone ostentatiously
__ 9.	**glitch**	i.	soft and limp
__10.	**gloss**	j.	to move about or play with something nervously

From the words above, fill in the blanks with the most appropriate word. (You may need to change the word form)

1. A _____ in the software made it impossible to log in.

2. The dead frog's body was limp, it's belly _____.

3. She couldn't hide her _____ at having won the award.

4. Maria was shy and never _____ her considerable accomplishments.

5. I was unconsciously _____ with my pen during the presentation.

6. He had worked himself into a _____ over a minor problem.

7. I could only _____ in astonishment when he told me the wonderful news.

8. The boy eventually learned not to _____ his parents' advice.

9. He was always _____ with his clients, which is why they all respected him.

10. This new paint has a high _____ finish that will make your car look good as new.

Review Exercise 13

Match the word with its definition.

___ 1. **gullible**   a. uncontrollably or irrationally emotional
___ 2. **haughty**   b. easily fooled, deceived or cheated
___ 3. **headstrong** c. pretend to possess virtues without having them
___ 4. **hierarchy**   d. a system that ranks people based on status
___ 5. **hoard**   e. stubbornly wilful and determined
___ 6. **hostile**   f. feeling or showing dislike or opposition
___ 7. **hypocrite**   g. to hint at or suggest something without saying it
___ 8. **hysterical** h. arrogantly superior and disdainfully proud
___ 9. **idiosyncrasy** i. a stock of resources that is hidden or guarded
___10. **imply**   j. a habit or trait that is unique to an individual

From the words above, fill in the blanks with the most appropriate word. (You may need to change the word form)

1. His main _____ was his ever-changing hair colour.

2. She is a _____ and never practices what she preaches.

3. He was as shrewd as his older brother was_____.

4. Instead of answering the interviewer's question, the Princess gave him a _____ smile and continued telling her story.

5. The child became _____ when he could not find his parents.

6. The crowd was unexpectedly _____ towards the speaker.

7. The Corporation had a clear and rigid _____.

8. She kept a secret _____ of candy in her drawer.

9. Some of the students were intimidated by her outspoken and _____ nature.

10. What do you think this sentence is trying to_____?

Review Exercise 14

Match the word with its definition.

  ___ 1. **incentive**   a. intended for or relating to young people
  ___ 2. **incongruous** b. lacking in brilliance, vitality or spirit
  ___ 3. **indigenous** c. something that motivates someone to act
  ___ 4. **inept**   d. to shout rude, mocking comments at someone
  ___ 5. **intrepid**   e. extremely happy and triumphant
  ___ 6. **irate**   f. having no skill or aptitude for something
  ___ 7. **jeer**   g. not in harmony with the surroundings
  ___ 8. **jubilant**   h. fearless and adventurous
  ___ 9. **juvenile**   i. extremely angry
  ___10. **lacklustre**   j. native to a particular place

From the words above, fill in the blanks with the most appropriate word. (You may need to change the word form)

1. I am tired of your _____ pranks.

2. The crowd _____ at her offensive remarks.

3. I finally have a strong _____ to learn French, since I am going to be in France for an year.

4. The visitor to the zoo asked whether the animals were_____ to the region.

5. The _____ explorers trekked through the dense jungle.

6. The football fans were _____ over their team's victory.

7. She had always been _____ at skiing, and kept falling over.

8. He was so _____ that his face was red, and his hands were shaking.

9. Her fiery words were _____ with her docile actions.

10. For all the hype it received in the media, the remake of the film was rather _____.

Review Exercise 15

Match the word with its definition.

__ 1.	**languid**	a. lack of energy or vitality
__ 2.	**lethargy**	b. subject to unpredictable changes in mood
__ 3.	**mercurial**	c. gloomy and ill-tempered
__ 4.	**moat**	d. relaxed and peaceful
__ 5.	**morose**	e. a water-filled trench surrounding a town or castle
__ 6.	**muddle**	f. to swing back and forth
__ 7.	**nuisance**	g. pleasant and acceptable, especially to the palate
__ 8.	**obdurate**	h. an inconvenient or annoying person or thing
__ 9.	**oscillate**	i. a disorganized, messy state
__10.	**palatable**	j. stubbornly resistant to outside influence

From the words above, fill in the blanks with the most appropriate word. (You may need to change the word form)

1. The king ordered a _____ to be built around his castle.

2. My family spent a nice _____ evening on the terrace.

3. I have been stuck in a feeling of _____ all day.

4. My feelings about leaving _____ between excited and nervous.

5. He was an entertaining albeit _____ character.

6. It is nearly impossible to cheer my sister up when she is in a _____ mood.

7. The emerging writer had learned to present his ideas in a more_____ way for the general public.

8. The two cats had left the living room in a terrible_____.

9. Our flight being delayed was a minor _____ for us.

10. No matter how much we tried to convince him to stay, he was _____ about quitting his job.

Review Exercise 16

Match the word with its definition.

__ 1. **placate**   a. having a heavy-set body
__ 2. **plight**   b. not held in place securely
__ 3. **porous**   c. having a preconceived negative opinion
__ 4. **portly**   d. a part viewed in relation to the other parts
__ 5. **potent**   e. powerful
__ 6. **pragmatic**   f. to make someone less angry
__ 7. **precarious**   g. full of pores
__ 8. **prejudiced**   h. dealing with things realistically
__ 9. **privation**   i. a lack of resources, necessities and comforts
__10. **proportion**   j. a difficult or unfortunate situation or state

From the words above, fill in the blanks with the most appropriate word. (You may need to change the word form)

1. Limestone is a _____ rock that lets water pass through.

2. Although Anna was initially _____ against him because of the rumours she had heard, she was happy to have been proven wrong.

3. The fermented cabbage had a surprisingly _____ smell.

4. It was not hard for me to empathize with their _____.

5. The poor man claimed that _____ was not a problem for him.

6. His daughter was the only one who knew how to _____ his anger.

7. She was very _____ about her finances and managed to save a lot.

8. He was a _____ gentleman with wide shoulders and a big goofy grin.

9. A career in show business is very _____.

10. I think they blew whole thing completely out of _____.

Review Exercise 17

Match the word with its definition.

__ 1. **prowess**   a. a state of uncertainty about what to do
__ 2. **qualm**   b. to give formal consent to something
__ 3. **quandary**   c. exceptional expertise or skill in a field
__ 4. **rash**   d. to tear down or demolish
__ 5. **ratify**   e. a feeling of worry or doubt about one's conduct
__ 6. **raze**   f. to recall the past
__ 7. **refute**   g. acting too hastily
__ 8. **relinquish**   h. to formally reject or abandon
__ 9. **reminisce**   i. to give up or surrender
__10. **renounce**   j. to prove a statement or theory false

From the words above, fill in the blanks with the most appropriate word. (You may need to change the word form)

1. I have no _____ about him taking over the project.

2. I love to _____ about our summers in the countryside.

3. He kept boasting about his athletic_____, but nobody had seen it in action.

4. Take the time to think through the details carefully, instead of making a _____ decision.

5. The fires _____ the forest to the ground.

6. No matter how much they threatened her, she would not _____ her beliefs.

7. To everyone's surprise, the king _____ the crown.

8. Luther was in a _____ about which job offer to accept.

9. The council members unanimously voted to_____ the new policy.

10. Our candidate expertly _____ every one of their opposing arguments.

Review Exercise 18

Match the word with its definition.

__ 1. **rue**   a. a soldier stationed to keep watch over a place
__ 2. **ruthless**   b. filled with unexpressed anger
__ 3. **salvage**   c. a fraud or hoax
__ 4. **scrupulous**   d. thinly scattered or distributed over an area
__ 5. **seethe**   e. criminal, evil or wicked
__ 6. **sentry**   f. to rescue
__ 7. **sham**   g. showing no pity, compassion or mercy
__ 8. **sinister**   h. cunning and deceitful
__ 9. **sly**   i. having morals and scruples
__ 10. **sparse**   j. a feeling of regret

From the words above, fill in the blanks with the most appropriate word. (You may need to change the word form)

1. Her seemingly earnest promise turned out to be a huge

   _____.

2. Karl was the very definition of a _____ old fox.

3. He will always _____ the day when he left her.

4. The _____ would not let anyone enter the palace.

5. There was something _____ about the way he was looking at us.

6. We try to live up to our reputation of being a _____ organization.

7. The old heiress was _____ in her pursuit of even more wealth.

8. She didn't know how to _____ that seemingly hopeless situation.

9. Instead of shouting, she stood at the back of room _____ with anger.

10. The trees on the mountain became increasingly _____ the higher up we climbed.

Review Exercise 19

Match the word with its definition.

___ 1. **splinter**   a. beneath the surface of the earth
___ 2. **squabble**   b. a small, thin and sharp piece of something
___ 3. **stampede**   c. gone or placed under the surface of water
___ 4. **stark**   d. a lie used to achieve a goal
___ 5. **steadfast**   e. to become less intense or violent
___ 6. **strive**   f. complete and utter
___ 7. **submerged**   g. to try very hard to reach a goal
___ 8. **subside**   h. firm and unchangeable
___ 9. **subterfuge**   i. a quarrel about something unimportant
___10. **subterranean**   j. a sudden, frenzied rush

From the words above, fill in the blanks with the most appropriate word. (You may need to change the word form)

1. The little boy had a _____ in his foot.

2. Even though they _____ often, they love each other very much.

3. You must _____ for the things you want.

4. His opponents were not above using _____ to achieve their ends.

5. The dark trees stood in _____ contrast to the pale, cloudy sky.

6. They remained _____ to their values.

7. As soon as the doors to the shop opened on the first day of the sale, we were almost trampled in the_____ of eager shoppers.

8. Several _____ tunnels run through the city.

9. My headache finally _____.

10. The submarines were _____ deep in the ocean.

Review Exercise 20

Match the word with its definition.

___ 1. **succumb**	a. having an unpleasant taste
___ 2. **swarm**	b. to take hold of power by force
___ 3. **thwart**	c. messy or dishevelled
___ 4. **toil**	d. to prevent from accomplishing a goal
___ 5. **tome**	e. a big group of flying insects, people or things
___ 6. **trench**	f. to yield or give way to a superior force
___ 7. **uniform**	g. a large, heavy scholarly book
___ 8. **unkempt**	h. a long, narrow ditch
___ 9. **unpalatable**	i. hard work
___ 10. **usurp**	j. a distinctive outfit

From the words above, fill in the blanks with the most appropriate word. (You may need to change the word form)

1. I rarely _____ to temptation.

2. They were attacked by a _____ of bees.

3. That soup was simply _____.

4. The king's brother failed in his attempt to _____ the throne.

5. The villain's evil plan was _____ by the hero and his friends.

6. Her job requires patience, determination and _____.

7. They were digging a _____ for a new water-pipe.

8. The homeless man was unwashed and_____.

9. The librarian brought out three _____ for me sift through.

10. I wish I did not have to wear this ugly _____ to work every day.

Review Exercise 21

Match the word with its definition.

___ 1. **vandalize**   a. fierce anger or vengeance
___ 2. **verbose**   b. to deface or destroy
___ 3. **verve**   c. to fade, shrivel and decay
___ 4. **vex**   d. speaking fluently without interruption
___ 5. **vigorous**   e. using too many words in writing
___ 6. **volatile**   f. to irritate or annoy
___ 7. **voluble**   g. a long journey
___ 8. **voyage**   h. liveliness and enthusiasm
___ 9. **wither**   i. changing suddenly and unpredictably
___ 10. **wrath**   j. forceful and energetic

From the words above, fill in the blanks with the most appropriate word. (You may need to change the word form)

1. I don't want to keep _____ you with silly questions.

2. They were running experiments with dangerously _____ chemicals.

3. _____ exercise a few times per week helps him stay in shape.

4. Nobody wanted to provoke her _____, so they kept quiet about the matter.

5. The _____ to the Moon was life changing for the astronauts.

6. The dancer moved across the stage with incredible vitality and_____.

7. If we don't pick the grapes immediately, they will _____ away on the vine.

8. The writer was asked to rewrite the paragraphs that were too _____ and ambiguous.

9. The boys got in trouble for _____ the walls of the building.

10. The_____ game show host was never at a loss for words.

Review Exercises Answers

Review Exercise 1

Matching

1.   c
2.   j
3.   e
4.   f
5.   g
6.   i
7.   h
8.   b
9.   d
10.   a

Fill in the Blanks

1.   accentuated
2.   acumen
3.   adorned
4.   aggravated
5.   accord
6.   aggrandize
7.   adamant
8.   acclaim
9   agile
10.   abduct

Review Exercise 2

Matching

1.   i
2.   g
3.   d
4.   h
5.   f
6.   b
7.   e
8.   j
9.   c
10.   a

Fill in the Blanks

1.   amassed
2.   ambiguous
3.   apex
4.   amble
5.   annulled
6.   anguish
7.   animated
8.   annihilated
9   aloof
10.   anomaly

Review Exercise 3

Matching

1.   i
2.   h
3.   g
4.   a
5.   d
6.   c
7.   e
8.   j
9.   b
10.   f

Fill in the Blanks

1.   aplomb
2.   arduous
3.   atoned
4.   applause
5.   assailed
6.   attire
7.   assemble
8.   astute
9   audible
10.   astonished

Review Exercise 4

Matching		Fill in the Blanks	
1.	b	1.	benefactor
2.	e	2.	bedraggled
3.	d	3.	benevolent
4.	h	4.	benign
5.	j	5.	barrage
6.	l	6.	besmirch
7.	f	7.	banquet
8.	g	8.	bastion
9.	a	9	basking
10.	c	10.	bias

Review Exercise 5

Matching		Fill in the Blanks	
1.	f	1.	callous
2.	d	2.	blandishment
3.	b	3.	capitulated
4.	j	4.	brazen
5.	i	5.	blemish
6.	e	6.	breach
7.	a	7.	bliss
8.	h	8.	castigate
9.	g	9	cache
10.	c	10.	bounty

Review Exercise 6

Matching		Fill in the Blanks	
1.	e	1.	catapult
2.	d	2.	chaos
3.	h	3.	commiseration
4.	b	4.	colossal
5.	i	5.	colluding
6.	f	6.	chandelier
7.	j	7.	celerity
8.	c	8	cease
9.	a	9	clemency
10.	g	10.	complacent

Review Exercise 7

Matching		Fill in the Blanks	
1.	b	1.	consent
2.	a	2.	deplore
3.	j	3.	confound
4.	g	4.	daunting
5.	i	5.	conjecture
6.	e	6.	concur
7.	h	7.	concave
8.	c	8.	debacle
9.	f	9	conundrum
10.	d	10.	conciliation

Review Exercise 8

Matching		Fill in the Blanks	
1.	b	1.	drenched
2.	e	2.	dexterous
3.	f	3.	dogma
4.	j	4.	domicile
5.	h	5.	eccentric
6.	g	6.	detest
7.	c	7.	deplore
8.	i	8.	deride
9.	d	9	disconnected
10.	a	10.	dogmatic

Review Exercise 9

Matching		Fill in the Blanks	
1.	h	1.	emulate
2.	c	2.	emaciated
3.	d	3.	egregious
4.	a	4.	elation
5.	g	5.	effrontery
6.	i/j	6.	eerie
7.	j/i	7.	ecstatic/elated
8.	e	8.	encrypt
9.	f	9	elated/ecstatic
10.	b	10.	edict

Review Exercise 10

Matching		Fill in the Blanks	
1.	i	1.	esteem
2.	b	2.	eroded
3.	h	3.	evade
4.	j	4.	endeavour
5.	f	5.	equitable
6.	e	6.	enhance
7.	d	7.	encumbered
8.	c	8.	enigmatic
9.	a	9	endorse
10.	g	10.	euphoric

Review Exercise 11

Matching		Fill in the Blanks	
1.	a	1.	expel
2.	j	2.	exulted
3.	h	3.	fastidious
4.	i	4.	exasperated
5.	c	5.	fealty
6.	e	6.	fawning
7.	f	7.	exalted
8.	d	8.	feat
9.	g	9	fickle
10.	b	10.	fallow

Review Exercise 12

Matching		Fill in the Blanks	
1.	j	1.	glitch
2.	i	2.	flaccid
3.	h	3.	glee
4.	g	4.	flaunted
5.	f	5.	fidgeting
6.	e	6.	frenzy
7.	d	7.	gape
8.	c	8.	flout
9.	b	9.	forthright
10.	a	10.	gloss

Review Exercise 13

Matching		Fill in the Blanks	
1.	b	1.	idiosyncrasy
2.	h	2.	hypocrite
3.	e	3.	gullible
4.	d	4.	haughty
5.	i	5.	hysterical
6.	f	6.	hostile
7.	c	7.	hierarchy
8.	a	8.	hoard
9.	j	9	headstrong
10.	g	10.	imply

Review Exercise 14

Matching		Fill in the Blanks	
1.	c	1.	juvenile
2.	g	2.	jeered
3.	j	3.	incentive
4.	f	4.	indigenous
5.	h	5.	intrepid
6.	i	6.	jubilant
7.	d	7.	inept
8.	e	8.	irate
9.	a	9	incongruous
10.	b	10.	lacklustre

Review Exercise 15

Matching		Fill in the Blanks	
1.	d	1.	moat
2.	a	2.	languid
3.	b	3.	lethargy
4.	e	4.	oscillated
5.	c	5.	mercurial
6.	i	6.	morose
7.	h	7.	palatable
8.	j	8.	muddle
9.	f	9	nuisance
10.	g	10.	obdurate

Review Exercise 16

Matching		Fill in the Blanks	
1.	f	1.	porous
2.	j	2.	prejudiced
3.	g	3.	potent
4.	a	4.	plight
5.	e	5.	privation
6.	h	6.	placate
7.	b	7.	pragmatic
8.	c	8.	portly
9.	i	9.	precarious
10.	d	10.	proportion

Review Exercise 17

Matching		Fill in the Blanks	
1.	c	1.	qualms
2.	e	2.	reminisce
3.	a	3.	prowess
4.	g	4.	rash
5.	b	5.	razed
6.	d	6.	renounce
7.	j	7.	relinquished
8.	i	8.	quandary
9.	f	9	ratify
10.	h	10.	refuted

Review Exercise 18

Matching		Fill in the Blanks	
1.	j	1.	sham
2.	g	2.	sly
3.	f	3.	rue
4.	i	4.	sentry
5.	b	5.	sinister
6.	a	6.	scrupulous
7.	c	7.	ruthless
8.	e	8.	salvage
9.	h	9	seething
10.	d	10.	sparse

Review Exercise 19

Matching

1.   b
2.   i
3.   j
4.   f
5.   h
6.   g
7.   c
8.   e
9.   d
10.   a

Fill in the Blanks

1.   splinter
2.   squabble
3.   strive
4.   subterfuge
5.   stark
6.   steadfast
7.   stampede
8.   subterranean
9   subsided
10.   submerged

Review Exercise 20

Matching

1.   f
2.   e
3.   d
4.   i
5.   g
6.   h
7.   j
8.   c
9.   a
10.   b

Fill in the Blanks

1.   succumb
2.   swarm
3.   unpalatable
4.   usurp
5.   thwarted
6.   toil
7.   trench
8.   unkempt
9   tomes
10.   uniform

Review Exercise 21

Matching

1.   b
2.   e
3.   h
4.   f
5.   j
6.   i
7.   d
8.   g
9.   c
10.   a

Fill in the Blanks

1.   vexing
2.   volatile
3.   vigorous
4.   wrath
5.   voyage
6.   verve
7.   wither
8.   verbose
9.   vandalizing
10.   voluble

Word List

abduct	astonish	catapult
accentuate	astute	cease
acclaim	atone	celerity
accord	attire	chandelier
acumen	audible	chaos
adamant	banquet	clemency
adorn	barrage	collude
aggrandize	bask	colossal
aggravate	bastion	commiseration
agile	bedraggled	complacent
aloof	benefactor	concave
amass	benevolent	conciliation
ambiguous	benign	concur
amble	besmirch	confound
anguish	bias	conjecture
animated	blandishment	consent
annihilate	blemish	conundrum
annul	bliss	daunting
anomaly	bounty	debacle
apex	brazen	deplore
aplomb	breach	deride
applause	cache	detest
arduous	callous	dexterous
assail	capitulate	disconcerted
assemble	castigate	dogma

dogmatic	exasperated	hysterical
doleful	expel	idiosyncrasy
domicile	exult	imply
drench	fallow	incentive
eccentric	fastidious	incongruous
ecstatic	fawning	indigenous
edict	fealty	inept
eerie	feat	intrepid
effrontery	fickle	irate
egregious	fidget	jeer
elated	flaccid	jubilant
elation	flaunt	juvenile
emaciated	flout	lacklustre
emulate	forthright	languid
encrypt	frenzy	lethargy
encumber	gape	mercurial
endeavour	glee	moat
endorse	glitch	morose
enhance	gloss	muddle
enigmatic	gullible	nuisance
equitable	haughty	obdurate
erode	headstrong	oscillate
esteem	hierarchy	palatable
euphoric	hoard	placate
evade	hostile	plight
exalted	hypocrite	porous

portly

potent

pragmatic

precarious

prejudiced

privation

proportion

prowess

qualm

quandary

rash

ratify

raze

refute

relinquish

reminisced

renounce

rue

ruthless

salvage

scrupulous

seethe

sentry

sham

sinister

sly

Sparse

splinter

squabble

stampede

stark

steadfast

strive

submerged

subside

subterfuge

subterranean

succumb

swarm

thwart

toil

tome

trench

uniform

unkempt

unpalatable

usurp

vandalize

verbose

verve

vex

vigorous

volatile

voluble

voyage

wither

wrath

Printed in Great Britain
by Amazon

11050627R00142